Remember the Creator

Also by William Wildblood

Meeting the Masters

978-1-78099-168-9 (Paperback)
978-1-78099-169-6 (ebook)

Remember the Creator

William Wildblood

AXIS MUNDI
BOOKS

Winchester, UK
Washington, USA

First published by Axis Mundi Books, 2019
Axis Mundi Books is an imprint of John Hunt Publishing Ltd., 3 East Street, Alresford, Hampshire
SO24 9EE, UK
office1@jhpbooks.net
www.johnhuntpublishing.com
www.axismundi-books.com

For distributor details and how to order please visit the 'Ordering' section on our website.

ISBN: 978 1 78535 927 9
978 1 78535 928 6 (ebook)
Library of Congress Control Number: 2017964336

A CIP catalogue record for this book is available from the British Library.

Design: Stuart Davies

Printed and bound by CPI Group (UK) Ltd, Croydon, CR0 4YY, UK
US: Printed and bound by Edwards Brothers Malloy 15200 NBN Way #B, Blue Ridge Summit, PA 17214, USA

Contents

Introduction

The title of this book comes from something I was told by my teachers many years ago. My previous book *Meeting The Masters* describes that experience. It is a phrase so simple as almost to pass unnoticed but I think it contains a key to the whole of the spiritual life. It's like a seed that can grow into a mighty tree if it is planted in fertile soil and correctly tended and watered.

The subject of this book is God. You might wonder what qualifications I have for writing about this, the subject of all subjects. Can I claim an intimate acquaintance? No. Have I encountered him? I can't really say so. Do I actually believe in him? Absolutely, and with all my heart. I believe in God and I believe that God is the ultimate fact, the one to which everything else must refer and without which nothing else makes any sense. I feel it is that which gives me the, I won't say right, but opportunity and maybe even, in this day and age, duty to write about him.

So, I shall be writing from the point of view of someone for whom the reality of God is a given. I may occasionally try to give rational reasons for believing in him but the fact is this world is set up in an extremely clever way in that there is not quite enough evidence to either believe or disbelieve if one goes solely by outer facts accessible to unsupported reason or logic. There is enough to indicate God but not enough to conclusively prove him so we have to make the leap of faith or, as I would rather put it, we have to respond on a different level to that of mere reason. It's a kind of test of our ability to transcend the self-centred mind and listen to the heart though, there is, of course, a right and wrong way to do this. That's why it is traditionally said that faith is a matter of the will rather than the intellect.

This book derives in part from articles written online for Meeting the Masters and Albion Awakening though these have been edited and expanded, and there are new pieces, too. I hope that, despite its multiple origins, the reader finds enough of a connecting thread to give it a cohesive unity.

Preface

The subject of God is one that has exercised human beings for as long as we know. In fact, it certainly goes back further than recorded history. No doubt as soon as we were able to think, this is what we thought about. Where did we come from? What made us? Indeed, what are we? But it would be a mistake to imagine that early human beings thought and felt as we do. Both their outer and inner worlds were different to ours. Their mode of consciousness was different to ours in that it participated in its surroundings. It was not separate from its immediate environment as is ours. So I think we can assume that early man lived in close communion with his gods. He didn't understand them but he knew they were there. Of course, these gods were not God, though even God may have been felt as an undercurrent to life, and so to begin with we just knew we were part of God and part of life though we had no clear comprehension of what that really meant. It just was what was.

As time went by, the world changed and so did we. Connection to the spiritual world receded and it was no longer perceived as the backdrop to the material world. We sought to recapture that and religions of various types arose. More time passed and the material world loomed ever more significantly in our consciousness but so did something else. That was an awareness of ourselves as separate individuals. Our minds began to develop. Our powers of rational thought began to assume a greater importance and we no longer just passively felt life. We began actively to think about it.

And so we have ended up here. We are now living at a time when the spiritual world has more or less completely receded from our consciousness and we are well and truly locked inside our own separate minds. This is the time when we have to turn around and start to recapture a spiritual focus. We have to step outside our own little minds into the greater world and from thence we have to start to build a relationship with God, our Creator. By this means we will eventually become godlike ourselves as we shift from a purely passive awareness of life to a more active engagement with it, albeit one in which attention is all on self, and then on to a creative and fully conscious union with it but not just with life as an impersonal, universal force. As we progress we will find that life is actually intensely personal, and that the reason for our creation in the first place was love. God created us because of love, because he is love, and the goal of the spiritual path is not simply to transcend the material world and rest in a pure non-dual consciousness but to reach a union in love with the Creator. The One became Many in order to know the joys of relationship. That is why God created us, and why he created us with free will.

In the Beginning

In 1978 I was adrift in a world that made no sense to me. I was 22 years old with no purpose in life because life offered nothing that answered the questions I had inside me which I could barely formulate but which boiled down to a search for meaning. But there was no meaning. There was be born, go to school, get a job, get married, get a family, work and die. That was more or less it. You could supplement it with music, art, entertainment and sex but none of those offered more than transitory escapes from the grim reality of a meaningless existence.

I was ripe for conversion. The cynic would say that I was open to any illusion that would offer me some escapist comfort, and one cannot deny that some people do turn to religion for just this reason but I was not of that sort. I was not seeking a faith or belief system in which I could feel at home, or any kind of outer thing, which is what those often are. I was searching for something which properly answered the lack of meaning I experienced in the world, and this had to be something real which truly went beyond appearances. Indeed, reality was what it was all about. There was no reality in the world I knew. It was a pale, lifeless imitation of that, though it appeared to satisfy most people. Few of my acquaintances seemed to bother with a search for something deeper than what was on offer. Presumably they had all considered whether there might be a God but had all decided against it, on the grounds of the apparent feebleness of contemporary religion and the seemingly confident claims of science that it had shown a materialistic view of life to be the only intelligent option. This did not seem to bother them and they just got on with their lives. I couldn't do that. If life really was no more than what my contemporaries assumed it to be then there was no point to it.

But precisely because I felt so strongly that there would be no point to a life lived according to the doctrine of materialism, I knew that had to be wrong. You don't feel a desperate need for something that doesn't exist. You just don't. Therefore there had to be something. But what? The Christianity of my upbringing, or at least my understanding of it, with its external God and its tedious (I'm afraid to say) representatives and its conventionalisms that mostly went along with everyday society had nothing to say to me. It was just so flat and uninspiring. Perhaps it was a case of over-familiarity but I think it was also a case of the religion having largely settled down into an accommodation with this world and, most of all, a failure to understand the true spiritual nature of the soul.

By that I mean that ordinary Christianity seemed to take the human being at face value. We were just what we seemed. Certainly, we needed salvation but we were not already spiritual beings who had forgotten their true home and come down to Earth. This world was our home, and what we seemed to be was what we were. Christ was outside us, and a long way off. There really was not that much difference between a believer and a non-believer in terms of what we were. They only disagreed about a future destination.

Now I realise that this is not what Christianity really teaches once you get to grips with it properly. But it is more or less the way it appeared, even to someone who had more than a passing acquaintance with its dogmas and doctrines. It was largely the way it presented itself.

The other major problem with contemporary religion was that it ignored or denied all the insights of the imagination. These were either dangerous and to be avoided or else they were simply false. But the imagination was essential to me at that time. It was the only thing I knew of that went beyond the dull facade of this world. It opened the mind up to something beyond outer appearance, but I had to accept this was not real because that was what we were told then. Imagination is just imagination. It can paint pretty pictures for our entertainment and even be very moving when it creates art, but none of that alters the mundane nature of the really real. It doesn't mean anything.

That's what I was led to believe by my upbringing and education. It's apparently what most people assume today. It is complete nonsense. Imagination, true imagination rather than the simple rearranging of thoughts and images that often goes by that name, is the forerunner of real intuitive knowing. It is the first flickering of direct vision into reality which sees and knows all in one movement. It is really a spiritual faculty rather than a mental one for it does not derive from prior sensual input, even though that can give it its form. Although it should not replace religion (when it does you can get into all sorts of trouble) it should certainly supplement it, for just as imagination without proper religious structure can lead to illusion and fantasy so religion without imagination is dry and exterior, and cannot sustain the spirit.

Although I didn't realise it, my concern with the imagination meant I was searching for God.

First Steps

I have told the story elsewhere of how I met someone in a metaphysical bookshop in London, who initially opened my young mind up to the reality of the spiritual world. But, briefly, this person was in his early sixties and had been at one time a Benedictine monk before later exploring Buddhism and Indian spirituality with the Ramakrishna mission. A typical spiritual dilettante, you might think, who had hopped from one thing to another but never stayed anywhere long enough to go deeply into anything. But that was not the case. He was a genuine seeker who had been unable to find a spiritual home. He was, and remained until the end of his life, a Christian but he could not completely reconcile any outer approach with his inner feelings, something I think that is more and more common today. Now we have the opportunity to explore many different kinds of spirituality, which is surely to our advantage, but I wonder if it is an unalloyed good. In the past there was usually just one approach to spirituality so that was the way we would have taken. Now, with everything on offer, there is a tendency for confusion and the dissipation of energy in several different directions. Swings and roundabouts, I expect, but even so when there is too much on offer we might miss the spiritual truth behind forms because of a preoccupation with all the different forms, and an attempt to match them up to each other. It can become a little academic.

This meeting set my life on a new course. It gave it a purpose and direction that had been lacking because it introduced me to the inner side of spirituality whereas before I had only been aware of its outer aspects. I won't repeat here what I wrote in my previous book but I should say that eventually it turned out that the person I had met, Michael Lord by name, was a medium and able to act in this capacity for spiritual beings who showed themselves to be wise and profound teachers, as well as thoroughly conversant with my personal shortcomings and the lessons I needed to learn.

I am aware of the problems with channelling as it is called now, though I tend to resist that description in my case as it is so often associated with communications which largely come from discarnate beings in what Christians would call purgatory or limbo but who imagine themselves to be in higher realms and speak accordingly. However, the baby and bathwater analogy applies here, and it would be a shame if faithful Christians rejected all spiritual contacts merely because some, or even most, come from dubious sources. Believing nothing is as mistaken as believing everything, and if one is sensible and subjects the fruits of any contact to the light of Christ, one should be well placed to extract some benefit from them.

At the same time, despite my experiences, I would not advise anyone to place too much confidence in any message or teaching received mediumistically. Always exercise discrimination and know that even if the source is genuine, in that it is not a demon or a product of the medium's own mind, it may well be overestimating its own spiritual stature. The realms beyond this mortal one are vast and can incorporate spirits of great intellect who are nonetheless still separate from God and whose metaphysical understanding, though "spiritual", may yet reflect that probably unacknowledged or even unrecognised separation.

We can therefore posit various forms of channelling. This excludes all fakes and frauds as well as the phenomenon of mediumistic contact with thought forms or clouds of psychic energy floating around on higher planes, which probably accounts for a large percentage. But when the channelling is real the source might come from:

- The recently dead such as are contacted in spiritualistic séances. These rarely have much of interest to communicate since they are ordinary souls with little spiritual experience or insight. The messages are usually also confused and inconclusive because of the difficulties of communication.

- Demons that come through deliberately to mislead and/or to absorb energy from those that fall prey to their machinations. Orthodox religion would put all in this category and point to various Biblical prohibitions, but when spiritual visitations and phenomena happen in the lives of the saints it is more forgiving. Having said that, no doubt a number of communications truly are demonic in origin so we should not go to the other extreme of gullible naivety with regard to such things.
- Souls that have made some progress up through the spiritual planes. Bear in mind that after death we have the opportunity to rise through the spiritual worlds as we throw off attachments pertaining to lower levels and identify more with aspects of our being that relate to higher ones. From our perspective in this material world, souls might appear to have great wisdom because they are speaking with knowledge of higher planes of existence and awareness of the wholeness of life and the reality of God. And yet they might still be on the outside looking in from the even higher perspective of a soul that has become one with God and fully realised its Christ nature.
- Souls that have realised their Christ nature in its fullness. In these souls the light of Christ has been born and grown and now completely illuminates their entire being. They have died with Christ and risen with him. They have become men and women made perfect and thus transcended the purely human kingdom to become members of the kingdom of heaven. In them, the process of theosis has reached its culmination. Their minds are irradiated with the wisdom of God and their hearts afire with his love.

> They are fully individual but one with all life having consciously united in themselves both matter and spirit to become a new creation.

Practically all channelling comes from sources one – three. But, to confuse matters, many claim to come from source four, whether because of deliberate deception or because some souls that have achieved a certain amount of post-mortem spiritual awakening genuinely believe themselves to have attained a fuller state of understanding than they actually have. That happens in this world and souls that have a tendency to over-estimate themselves and their spiritual status will probably continue to do so after death until they learn better. I do believe that there are some communications from source four but they are very rare. You must judge these things by their fruits and by the tone of the communication, how it strikes the heart and how it elevates and purifies the mind. Souls from source four do try to communicate with their disciples in this world but they chiefly do so by spiritual means, that is to say through the intuition. Their aim is to bring their pupils up to where they themselves are, which is why, for the most part, they work on the level of the spiritual soul rather than the earthly mind.

Obviously, I cannot prove that the beings who spoke to me through Michael came from source four but I do think that anyone who reads their words, as recorded in the book I wrote about the experience, should be able to sense a little of their authority. As far as I am concerned, they were members of the kingdom of heaven, part of that throng of spirits who are one with God and who comprise humanity's best saints and sages. They taught me in this way on and off for about 20 years, a lot at first, less as time went by as they are not ones to spoon-feed and it was assumed I had the sense to learn from them without the need to have the teaching reinforced by constant repetition. I am genuinely puzzled as to why they took what must have been quite a lot of trouble over me. But I suppose this dedication of service to their juniors is what distinguishes a real saint. As they themselves told me, **"Sometimes the less evolved can only advance through the loving sacrifice of the more evolved."**

Looking back, I would say that the chief lesson I learned from them was the reality of God. They did not speak of God that much but they demonstrated his reality in themselves. They also told me to think of them as messengers from God, which I did and do. God sends his messengers to us in many forms, and though it may be in a direct way like this, that is by no means usually the case. We have to learn to keep our spiritual eyes and ears open. For a long time I didn't speak of them to anyone (except Michael, of course) and that was not only because I assumed most people would think I was naive, gullible, stupid or mad but because to speak of them while they were still speaking to me would have seemed a kind of profanation. I can't explain it better than that. If they had suggested I should speak of them to others, then naturally, I would have done so, but they didn't so I kept silent.

Since Michael died and they no longer speak to me in any outer sense, I feel it not only legitimate but right to talk of the experience. I am certainly not their ambassador but I have had the huge benefit of being talked to by genuine spiritual beings and it makes sense to share that, however amateurishly, in this benighted age. For I can confirm that such beings really do exist and in themselves are the nearest thing to a concrete proof of a loving Creator we could expect, short of personal revelation.

The Masters

In my book *Meeting the Masters* I tried to describe the nature of the spiritual beings who spoke to me. I wish I could do them justice but my powers of description fall short. They inspired both love and respect, even a certain amount of awe, in me and I don't consider myself as someone easily impressed. Over the course of my life I have met all sorts of people but none of them could hold a candle to the Masters. Michael, who had led a very sophisticated life mingling with aristocracy and political leaders on the one hand, and film stars and celebrities on the other, said the same thing. He did not speak to them as I did (naturally, since he was their medium) but they communicated with him clairaudiently and he told me he sometimes saw faces of great beauty and dignity. He had met people from Winston Churchill to Mahatma Gandhi, and all sorts and conditions of men and women in between. No one, he said, could begin to compare to the Masters.

This was not because of anything as mundane as charisma or force of personality, "star quality." Michael had met plenty of people like that and knew it was usually a fairly superficial thing. No, it was to do with spiritual presence, an aura (for want of a better word) of love and wisdom that imposed by its certainty and depth rather than a feeling of power or excitement. Power there was in plenty but it was the power of truth not personality, and it was accompanied by a sense of peace like no other. I am not comparing the Masters with Christ, though I do think of them as something like his disciples, but I was often reminded of the words from the Gospel of St John when they spoke. "My peace I give unto you." Sometimes they used almost the exact same words, usually on departure when they blessed me, and the peace they bestowed during and after a visit was an almost tangible thing. For a while at least, until the afterglow of their presence faded and I was back in the everyday world.

I think their words as reported in the book from notes I took at the time (alas, I only did so for the first year) convey something of their quality. But they don't give a feel of their presence which taught as much as the words they spoke. To me they seemed of another world but not in the sense of being inhuman. They were very human but had all the virtues of the ideal man with none of the shortcomings of the mortal version. They had developed in themselves all the spiritual qualities, love, wisdom and so on, but had these in a real and inbuilt sense not in the rather self-conscious way one often encounters them in spiritual circles. It was how they were, as natural to them as thought and emotion are to us. They radiated a feeling of total authenticity, and also a nobility that imposed by its authority and absolute truthfulness. But they never enforced this.

The difference between these spiritual beings and any person in this world striving to be spiritual, even the best of us, is profound. I have said the Masters were very human and so they were but they were also much more than human. They came from another place, one in which the possibility of sin or falseness was entirely absent, and where love was the dominant mode of being, a pure and holy love bearing little resemblance to our rather crude, often tainted by ego, versions of it. They walked in the light of God, and felt and thought in a way that was completely centred in the reality of God. For them God was a constant presence and a fact from which everything else derived.

I have been asked how many of them spoke to me. The truth is I don't exactly know. The answer is several and I could usually tell one from another but no names were given except once, when one of the higher Masters spoke to me. That was how he was introduced by another Master who had spoken to me earlier in the session. He had an air of such regality that I felt, even more than usual, that I had better be on my best behaviour. I must repeat that this was neither asked nor expected of me. It was simply the natural authority of their presence that prompted such a reaction in me. The higher Masters did not speak to me often but I mention them to make the point that even in heaven there is hierarchy. And why would there not be? If spiritual evolution (as in unfoldment of pre-existing potential, similar to the development from seed to tree) is endless, and I think it is, that is only to be expected. This, by the way, is a crucial difference between theistic and non-theistic forms of religion or mysticism. When you reach enlightenment or realisation in the latter, that's more or less it. You have reached the absolute and where is there to go after that, especially if there is no "I" to go anywhere? But a theistic system in which the One and the Many both exist has the possibility of there being endless vistas of reality, deeper and deeper truths as you enter ever more completely into the heart of God and the fullness of truth. And God has no top nor bottom nor beginning nor end to him at all.

I have also been asked why, given such beings as Masters exist, they do not communicate with more people more frequently but this is to misunderstand their purpose. The Masters are spiritual teachers in the purest sense and that is why they do not teach through words, which are concrete things that may obscure as much as they convey, so much as through influence. Their aim is to make their disciples receptive to the spiritual plane of being, not the idea of the spiritual plane, and their primary focus is on awakening the intuition. This they do by stimulating the so-called higher bodies and then encouraging the disciple to, metaphorically speaking, stretch upwards beyond the everyday mind (through meditation, aspiration, self-forgetfulness, prayer and the like), and thereby become more attuned to the soul. There are plenty of teachers in this world to do the still important but more preliminary work of reorienting those focused in their earthly selves to the soul, but the work of the Masters lies with those who are already conscious of the soul as the dominating force in their lives but have not as yet become fully one with it. That is why they work predominantly on higher, super-sensory levels.

You can get an idea of their teaching methods by considering their own words.

Obey the impressions we fill you with and be true to yourself. The more you respond to impression, the stronger it will become.

Note their choice of words as well as what they say. They use the word "obey." Obedience goes against the grain for the modern person as it appears to challenge our personal autonomy, and we are very self-centred people. We are individuals and we demand our freedom. But we are not free. We are slaves to the ego with its self-will, opinions and desires. Spirituality requires surrender and submission to the higher authorities, our teachers and our own soul. It requires obedience. Here's a novel definition of a Master for you. It is one who is perfectly obedient. Obedience makes us free.

The Elusiveness of God

I was very fortunate in that I was given something quite close to living proof of the reality of God. Spiritual beings of great love and wisdom who described themselves as his messengers came and spoke to me. But most of us are not so fortunate. Many people yearn for a sign from God but it is not forthcoming, not in a direct and obvious way certainly.

So often people ask, in varying degrees of frustration, how can God, if he is really there, not be apparent? If he is the Supreme Being and the foundation of all that is, how can it be that we are completely unaware of him and there is no sign of him either inside our minds or out there in Nature? No definite irrefutable sign anyway. This is such an important subject representing, as it does, a stumbling block to so many that it must be addressed by anyone who proclaims that belief in God is largely a moral matter, a question of will just as much as faith or intellect.

The first and obvious point to make is that the brain is a physical thing and, under normal conditions, it cannot receive input from non-physical levels. God is not a physical being. Though he is present in physical matter (or else it could not be) he, in himself, is spiritual. Please note that I am saying "he" but I am not at the moment concerned with arguing for the personal or impersonal nature of the absolute, though my stance on that score will be plain. Here I just use the word God to mean the spiritual truth behind the manifested universe and the source of everything real.

The second point is that it is perhaps we who have cut ourselves off from an awareness of God or spiritual life. By identifying ourselves exclusively with ourselves, we have descended further into matter. We have turned our backs on God because we have focused on our own little self as it is known by the mind, and the more we have done that, the more we have created a false reality for ourselves. I am not saying that we create our own reality (that's obviously not the case, there is an objective, phenomenal reality) but our mind can distort reality to reflect its own preconceptions and that is what we have done in this instance. We have identified with a particular type of mentally based consciousness, and that has cut out God who can only be known when we are not identified with the individual self.

And then there is another point. Why are we in this world? What is it that we are here to do? Let us assume the reality of God, which is fair enough when one is asking why we can't perceive him if he is there. So, assuming God exists, why does he send us to this material world instead of leaving us safe and sound in spiritual bliss? It can only be for us to develop in ways that would not be possible in spiritual bliss. The fact is that if you knew God was there, absolutely knew because you could see it, then you could not develop real goodness yourself because that comes from making the decision, which must be freely made, to love and trust God and to consciously put yourself on his side. This decision can only be made when the fact of God is not present to make it for you. You have to consciously embrace goodness and truth when their opposite is present. Indeed, you have to consciously embrace those things when they are hard to embrace in order for them to be part of you.

All human beings are potentially aware of God. The knowledge of God is in the very fabric of our being. The presence of spirit is clearly perceptible in Nature too. However, if we are to learn what we should while in this world then we must, to an extent, be cut off from higher realities, which realities we must then recapture by our own efforts. This is clearly a risk, and separation from the source can be taken too far, as seems to have happened in the modern world, but for God, who wants his children to grow up and become more and more like him rather than be slaves or automata, it is a risk worth taking, and who is to say that he doesn't have fail safe mechanisms built into the system?

This matter of God's absence, or apparent absence, is of enormous importance because resolving it could determine how we lead our lives. It could even determine how we end our lives and what happens thereafter. It's probably the greatest question there is. So it's worth considering at greater length. After all, practically everyone must have asked themselves at some point why, if God exists, is he not plainly visible or, at least, why is his presence not manifest in some way? Where is he? Let's try and answer that question.

There are actually several answers to this depending on where you are coming from. To begin with you can just reject the question and say that God's presence is clear if you look properly. It is clear internally, from the fact of your being, your consciousness and your individuality. All these things speak a divine reality. None of them can be explained by a strictly materialistic conception of the world. They all involve something more than what can be measured or perceived by the senses, and individuality, the sense of "I", actually requires a prototype, a divine I AM. The Buddhist idea that it is just an assemblage from component parts, that the whole is less than the sum of its parts, makes materialistic assumptions about a metaphysical reality and does not go anywhere near deep enough. You can apply a Buddhist line of reasoning to effectively deconstruct the separate ego but not individuality *per se,* because that is not a phenomenal thing so it is not open to purely rationalistic analysis.

But if that is not enough then the reality of God is clear from the outer world, too. First of all, that there is one at all, that there is something rather than nothing. I know modern science tries to explain this by various means but the order of improbability that everything, or anything, has arisen out of nothing is so infinitely huge that it could only be believed by someone who already wanted to believe it.

And then the reality of God is clear from the order in the

world, from the fact that it is not just chaos (in which case we could not know it at all) but has laws, regular patterns and what you might call a flexible design. By this I mean there is a mixture of design and freedom and it's hard to tell where one leaves off and the other starts. This is precisely what one would expect from a Creator who does not just make things in a rigid, sterile and mechanical way but builds freedom into his creation so that it might, as it were, co-create itself from within. This makes it much more interesting to God but it also confuses us for we expect one thing or another not a dynamic mix of the two: freedom and necessity. But, as I say, that is just what one would expect from a truly creative spirit who wants what he creates to participate in its own creation.

The reality of God is also made known by the beauty in the world and the fact of its fundamental goodness. To be sure, it is not perfect but the badness in it, as in us, comes from good things gone wrong. It is not a principle in itself any more than destruction can take place without creation preceding it. If beauty and goodness do not speak of a Creator to you then it's hard to know what could, but the difficulty may be that we simply take them for granted and thus fail to see the evidence they provide of God's existence. We are too used to them. That they are not all there is in the world is irrelevant. It just means that the world is not perfect, but then, why should it be? Perhaps that is not its *raison d'être,* and it does not exist for its own end but for the fulfilment of a greater purpose.

Obviously nothing I have said here will convince anyone but the already convinced. But that is the point really. God's presence is there if you wish to see it, but not if you don't. There is just enough evidence for him if you are willing to make a (relatively small) leap of faith but not enough if you are not. Why should faith be important? I think it must be because faith is the sign of acceptance that there is something more than just you as you seem to be and the world out there as it is in appearance. It is an opening up of yourself to the greater truth of spirit, and if you are to know spirit in a conscious and participatory way then you must be willing to know it. You must go towards it, and that is faith.

That is one way of approaching this question. It's not a serious question because God's presence is not hidden if you are looking properly. But I admit this is a bit unfair. Most of us are not looking properly because we don't know how to do that. And even then you could justifiably say that God's presence might be indicated or implied but it is not so obvious that there can be no dispute about it. The Creator is not right before our eyes in the way that the creation is. Why is this? Why would he hide in this way or, at least, not reveal himself? But there are answers to this, too.

The first thing to say is that perhaps God is not hiding from us. It is we who have separated ourselves from him. Our original connection to God was lost at the event, or through the process, known as the Fall as described in the book of Genesis. It was lost by our turning away from God and towards our own selves. We abandoned God for ego. You cannot have both, since the former is oneness and the latter is separation. God was known to us as long as we were true to the fundamental laws of being, but when we turned from those in search of our own fulfilment then we cut ourselves off from him. This resulted, so the story goes, in death and suffering which may not have been a necessary part, or so necessary a part, of our spiritual development otherwise. This is not a punishment but an inevitable consequence of our listening to the voice of the separate self.

But then there is this. God wants us to be free and full individuals for only as such can we share in his life and his creativity. And only individuals can love. Separation leads to the development of self which could not happen if we were constantly surrounded by God's presence. We would be unable to grow as individuals and develop our own unique quality if we did not have the freedom so to do, and we would not have this freedom if God's presence were always before us. There would be no real choice, no room to exercise free will properly. So God withdraws to give us the freedom to grow and, hopefully, eventually start to look for him ourselves. But in so doing we have to stretch ourselves upwards as seeds in the ground do towards the sun, and by doing that we grow spiritually because we rise to meet God on his own level rather than, as before, in the days when we had not fully separated out from life, meeting him where we already were.

Thus you can say that we have to leave home in order to return to it and recognise it in a new and higher way. Before we can truly see that subject and object are ultimately one in their essence we have to experience them as separate. But does this mean the Fall was intended? I think not. I think that our spiritual evolution would have involved a lot less suffering if the Fall had not occurred in the way it did. There might still have been a kind of separation but not as complete as the one that took place. The pain of evil might not have bitten so hard. Suffering and death might not have come in the way they did. But God is able to bring good out of ill so he uses the spiritual disaster of the Fall to effect a deeper redemption but one that now requires the incarnation and sacrifice of Christ to come about.

I hope it can now be seen why it is that the fact of God is not obvious to us. This is a fallen world and we have fallen with it. But it is also a place of learning, not a garden of paradise and if we are to be full and free individuals then we must become so on our own. Just as children must separate themselves in consciousness from their parents to grow up properly, so we must know separation from our divine parent if we are ever to approach him on his own level and in his own likeness and so eventually become like him. For early man may have been one with nature but he was not one with the Creator in a fully conscious sense. The path of spiritual evolution exists to enable him to accomplish this, and eventually build a full relationship with his Creator based on love and, if not equality, a kind of reciprocity. It is the means whereby a spiritual infant becomes a spiritual adult.

Evidence for God

There are then good reasons for God's apparent absence from the world, but still, I think, most people would instinctively tend to believe in him were it not for the fact that they are told by those they consider more qualified than themselves that there is no evidence. Professionals, scientists and philosophers have looked but not found and they can't all be wrong, can they? We used to believe in God but that was before we had modern science to explain what we are and how we've evolved from the primeval soup. Progress has shattered the myth of a divine creator. Now we know better.

To which one would reply that there is actually plenty of circumstantial evidence for God from religion, revelation, tradition, intuition, form and quality of the world, sense of goodness, love and beauty and so on but, admittedly, there is no material evidence. But then why should there be?

What people mean by no evidence is evidence that would convince them on a physical or mental level, scientific evidence, but that is a strange thing to expect of a spiritual being or of spirit *per se* which by definition is immaterial.

If reality is spiritual how could it be detectable to beings functioning only through their material selves? If there is a Creator why would we expect to see him in his creation, as though he were part of creation? He may be within it as its being but, in himself, he is outside it, transcendent to it.

God is not an object of knowledge. He is not a thing to be known as one knows created things, as one thing among others. He is not a being as we are but Being itself. This means he can only be known through being; that is, through becoming him or realising him within oneself. However, that is a purely spiritual knowledge which can be grasped intuitively but is not known through the rational mind.

If we want to know God through our minds, we are asking the impossible. It simply cannot be done because the mind is a material thing. You cannot know spirit through matter. You cannot prove the reality of spirit on a material level or in ways that convince a material being. Any God that could be known by or proved to the mind as we currently conceive it would not be a true God but some other created being with a created form and nature. So the fact there is no material or outer evidence for God rather counts in his favour.

But there is another reason that there is no direct proof of God in this world. If there were it would make it much harder for us to grow up spiritually. We need to let go of God's hand to find him within ourselves and start the process of inner transformation that develops the spiritual seed within us. We are forced to reach within and begin to stand on our own spiritual feet. In doing so we expand our horizons and develop spiritual qualities in a way that would not be possible in a situation in which there existed no choice as to the reality of God. This way we make our spirituality our own and not something that is, as it were, applied to us from without like a coat of paint.

So be grateful there is no proof of God. I wouldn't go so far as to say that very fact constitutes a proof but if I did it would not be an entirely ridiculous thing to say. I do say, though, that the absence of material proof is precisely what gives us the opportunity to become truly spiritual ourselves. By having to reach up to God we develop our own spiritual muscles and can become more like him in a way that would not be possible if he came down to us on the level at which we currently find ourselves. We have to stretch to grow.

If you are asking for evidence for God, then you simply don't understand what God is. He is not a thing. As I said above, he is not an object. Having said that, there is one very solid piece of evidence for God and that is you yourself. Yes, you are the proof of God. You, a person, a unique individual with free will and consciousness, a sense of right and wrong and a feeling for truth and beauty. You are the living proof of God, you and the sense of "I am" within you. For your "I am" is nothing less than the true image of God, the imprint of God stamped into your being. I AM is God.

Spirit and Matter

We have talked about spirit and matter but not really defined these words in any way. I actually rather like not defining them as a definition limits them in a way that leaving their interpretation open to the imagination does not. For we all understand, or should do, what spirit and matter are, even if we cannot plumb the depths of what they are. We sense that each describes a very different aspect of life. That, roughly speaking, spirit is life and matter the garb spirit takes on to express itself. An intellectual analysis can certainly elucidate that basic idea to a degree but it can also unnecessarily complicate it, and, worse, lock one up in theory which is self-defeating since mind, a material thing insofar as thought is expressed in form, can never comprehend spirit which is intuited or known directly. The annals of philosophy are full of highly intelligent people picking over the bones of a corpse. But still, we are intellectual beings so one should make some attempt to expand on a basic definition while stressing that words can obscure the truth as much as they can help to uncover it.

I am regarding spirit as the essence of life and matter as the substance through which that essence manifests itself: the inner and outer components of being. But while the modern world accepts matter as the stuff of which we are made (though it's getting harder and harder to know exactly what that is) it denies spirit, regarding it, if existing at all, as arising from material forces. This is the basis of materialism, that matter comes before consciousness which is secondary. Naturally, I disagree with that. Of course I do. It's wrong! So, what is spirit?

One way to think of spirit is as the energy of pure being which animates otherwise inert matter thus enabling the one to become many, and the whole universe of becoming, change, time, space and so on to appear. But the word "energy" can mislead for spirit is not some impersonal force like a cosmic gas spread throughout the universe, and I doubt could have been conceived of as such before the rise of materialistic science which effectively transposed its concepts onto the spiritual plane. Spirit is fully and gloriously personal, though it may have a non-personal aspect. For it is life and life is consciousness and consciousness requires one who is conscious. I AM implies an I. And an I implies a mind.

So spirit and matter are the basic duality of creation. They are expressed as life and form, subject and object, God and Nature and so on. This doesn't mean there is an irresolvable duality at the heart of existence, for ultimately these two are one. Whether you regard things theistically or not the position is the same. Either matter is an aspect of spirit projected out as the vehicle for its manifestation or God creates matter from nothing as the fundamental stuff from which he then forms everything else. Whichever way you look at it, matter either comes from spirit or is a part of it. But it is different to it as that which receives is different to that which gives. It is its complementary opposite in manifestation which is necessarily dualistic or nothing could be at all. Perfect oneness would be little different to perfect noneness.

Spirit and matter are the two poles of existence required for existence to be known. Matter is the mirror in which God is enabled to see his face and, as creation, it becomes his bride. Spirit is what gives life to matter, and the two combine to bring about all that is, with spirit working through matter, which includes time and space, to carry life onwards to unimaginable glories of ever greater truth and beauty, making the one many and the many more and more perfect individualised manifestations of the one. Without spirit, matter is dead. Without matter, spirit remains in darkness and alone, unable to see its face or express itself. They are two but they are also one and through their interaction the universe is born.

That is on the macrocosmic level. On the microcosmic level our task is to render the material portion of our being ever more receptive to the spiritual, which we do through the purification of mind and body, and the turning of our consciousness both inwards and upwards, not quite the same thing and both necessary. We have to transfer our attention from the phenomenal world and its contents to the spiritual one, and the priorities of the latter must become ours. It is a mistake to give too much attention to matter. It is, after all, not meant to be the primary partner in the relationship. But it is also a mistake to reject or ignore or downgrade it in any way since life is a relationship to which both partners contribute, just as both do to a dance. The expression of life in matter is the expression of love.

Spirit is the light and life of creation and matter its substance and foundation. From their union comes soul which gives being its quality.

God the Father

Now we have established that God exists, the next thing to do is to try to determine what sort of God he is. Earlier I spoke of God as "he" but didn't expand on that. Here I would like to develop that idea a little.

We live at a time when the differences between men and women are often dismissed as purely cultural with the implication, or even assumption, that there is no real difference between them other than the obvious physical ones, and even they are being questioned nowadays. Of course, anyone not led astray by the deviations of modernity, fomented by forces seeking to separate man from his Maker, knows this is not true, but it is hard for people to stand by their intuitions when they are bombarded by propaganda from the media telling them that these are misguided and invalid. And not just the media, for now the worlds of science and education have also both set their faces against spiritual truth. This, it must be emphasised, is a choice. It is not a rational attitude based on an objective interpretation of the universe. It is a deliberate decision to deny truth, if not at the lower, rank and file levels of those who follow where they are led, then certainly at the higher levels that actually run the show. There is an assault on spiritual reality at the present time (both by denying it and by perverting it) and one of the ways this agenda is pursued is by the deconstruction of the human form. If two things as radically different as man and woman are regarded as basically the same, then they are both cut off from deeper levels of their being, and their nature can be reassembled to specifically preclude any spiritual (or true spiritual as a false spirituality might well be added to the mix) content or awareness. In saying this, I am naturally not disputing that men and women are both the same as human beings, but I am upholding the reality of two different and complementary sexes and saying that this is all-important as it reflects an archetypal and divine truth. One that goes all the way back to the primal division of spirit and matter, as previously discussed.

This is why I regard modern feminism as one of the current weapons in the war against God. It is a sad thing when something presented as a good, and which certainly has some good aspects, is actually the opposite of that. I tend to believe that some of those who are deceived by this want to be deceived as they feel their personal agendas can be advanced by the deception. Nevertheless, even if they are willing victims, they are still victims. It might be countered that feminism has done much good by releasing women from their inferior roles and giving them opportunities they would never have had, but the good it may have done is more than offset by the harm it does as many women are derailed from their true vocation as women and denied access to the inner realities of femininity. In addition, the relation between the sexes is reduced from a loving complementarity to something that has become much more competitive. Besides, inferior role? That rather presupposes the truth of the feminist doctrine in the first place; that is to say, the assumption that the relation between men and women is best defined in terms of politics and equality. Obviously the past was far from perfect but it was an imperfect version of truth. We now appear to be aiming for a perfect lie. The fact that the relation between the sexes was often abused in the past to male advantage (though less so in Western cultures than some others) does not mean that the essential truth of two different sexes, each with its own role in the scheme of things, is wrong.

I say that feminism derails women from their true vocation as women for several reasons. Firstly, it gives them a false idea of themselves, of what they are and what they should be. I see this plainly as a man. It is a truth, clear in the light of the reality of God, which we should all be able to see if our vision had not been clouded by worldly propaganda. Wise women should be able to see it more clearly than me or any man. But so many women today can't see it or won't. And this brings me to the second point. Feminism cuts women off from their own source of inner wisdom. By emphasising traditionally masculine qualities and types of intellect, and promoting doing over being, it makes women think much more along analytical/mechanical lines and leaves them far less open to intuition and direct perception as traditionally they always have been. Women are being trained and encouraged to become more like men and less like women. They can't ever fully succeed in this, and they lose a lot by deforming themselves in the attempt to do so.

The inevitable effect of all this is that individuals live increasingly in a world of ideology and theory rather than reality and truth, and, as a consequence, become increasingly alienated from reality and truth. What is more, women are no longer able to provide a harmonious counterbalance to men to the mutual advantage of both, and the whole of humanity suffers. If we ask why this has been allowed to happen when it is clearly counter to the reality of what human beings are, a reality happily accepted for as long as we know, the answer is twofold. One, it has been encouraged by the dark forces who have their own agenda of spiritual destruction, and who know how to play on the sense of injustice. And two, it finds ready victims in materialistic times, with people motivated by rebellion against God, even if they don't perceive things in those terms. We should also not forget the elements of truth in feminism because there are some. It would never have caught on if that were not the case, but these really just sugar the pill.

I have taken rather a long time to come to the point but I wanted to set the scene before doing so. The point is, why is God called Father? Is this a mere convention or an accurate reflection of reality? Is it a "patriarchal" distortion of truth or does it really say something about the nature of the Supreme Being? I will affirm here that it is a correct description of God as Creator, one based on reality, and that is why I had first to set out my case against the chief proponent of the idea that it is just a convention which could easily be changed.

I will start with the fact that Christ called God the Father. Now there are many different religions and all contain elements of the truth but that does not mean that all are equally true. Given that they are descriptions of spiritual reality and spiritual reality is a) vast, and b) capable of ever deeper interpretation, we should expect that. Religions generally either come from the experience of an initiating teacher, as in Buddhism, or from revelation, and Christianity is the most recent revelation and the one that comes from the highest level. What about Islam, you might ask? Islam may have been chronologically more recent but it is really just a revamp of the Old Testament so it is metaphysically and spiritually less developed. The revelation of Christ, which includes the revelation of the Trinity, is the most profound revelation of spiritual truth humanity has received to date. I'm afraid you either see this or you don't, and if you don't you might consider what is stopping you. You could have a preference based on various factors, birth and background particularly, and that is fine. God has sent different religions to suit different types of people and all (all within reason) have the power to bring you to him, I believe. Nevertheless, as I stated earlier, they are not all equal, and Christ is the revealer of truth above all others, both in his teachings and, especially, in his person. I would also say that, though all religions have an understanding of the sacred, it is in Christianity that there is the greatest sense of the holy.

So the fact that Christ called God Father is important. He specifically referred to him in that way, and if you want to say that this was just a cultural matter, you have to explain why in so many other ways, including that of giving far more attention to women than earlier Jewish prophets, Christ went against the cultural norms of his time. You also would be disregarding the essence of who Christ was and denying that he had any real insights into spiritual reality.

But that is just my starting position. If Christ said one thing and all the evidence pointed in another way, that would create rather a large problem. But the fact is, it all points in the same way. If you have a philosophical conception of God as simple, unmanifest, pure spirit beyond Creation, there is not much you can say at all. All words fall back at the threshold of naked existence. But once we think of God as Creator, as something that acts and has a mind and a will, and, as created beings that is what we must do, then we see that he is indeed best described as Father and that the language of fatherhood sums up the relation of the Creator to creation better than any other. For, as we have seen, the name of God that most defines him is I AM. He is the supreme subject to which the whole of creation is object, and this takes us right to the roots of the masculine/feminine divide, showing us that it is there at the beginning of manifested being, where it reveals itself in subject and object. Now, clearly God is God and encompasses all things, so some of his qualities can be described in feminine terms, but if we are talking about his essence rather than his qualities, and if we are describing him as the Creator then he is masculine for he generates creation whether that be *ex nihilo* or from a feminine aspect that he projects from himself – prime matter, the receptive substance. But, at any rate, creation is generated by God not incubated in him, and, although an aspect of him is within it, in himself he remains transcendent to it. Similarly, all creation is receptive to him and he is positive to it. Consequently, although motherhood can certainly be used to describe some of the results of creation, it cannot be used of the initial and fundamental creative act.

None of this means there are not aspects of divine being that can manifest in feminine form. But the Supreme Being and Creator of the Universe is best understood as God the Father, just as taught by Jesus, and as demonstrated in a metaphysical sense by the fact that existence itself is, if it is anything, pure positivity.

To conclude, if considered as unexpressed being, God is neither masculine nor feminine because there are no manifested qualities in unexpressed being at all. It is a state of complete inactivity. But when considered as the personal God and Creator, he is masculine with the whole of Creation as his bride. And I am tempted to wonder whether this so-called impersonal aspect is not a creation of philosophers who have projected a theory into a reality. I don't dispute that something approximating to it might exist but is it the absolute, as sometimes postulated, or is it just an aspect of the personal God that remains unexpressed, the ground of being for instance? That is to say, is it a part of him rather than him being a part of it? For if it were the supreme state, how could the personal God ever have arisen? How could something have come from nothing if it were not already contained there? In which case, the impersonal would not really be the impersonal even in the absolute state. We shall consider these matters later. For the moment let us just say that the real essence of God is not to be found in What but in Who.

God as Father and Mother

One of the problems central to our time is the confusion relating to the male/female duality. This is so counter to Nature and to most people's instincts that it is not unreasonable to suppose that it is diabolically inspired or, at least, that something which was meant to take us forward in one direction has been hijacked and sent in another. But the main reason this confusion has been able to take any kind of effect at all, and not just be laughed out of court, is that we have no sense of metaphysics nowadays so no understanding that sex is not arbitrary or meaningless but something real that is the echo of a much higher truth. For the masculine/feminine duality goes right down to the heart of existence and it is present, in some form, from the very beginning.

In the past most monotheistic religions have downplayed, if not completely ignored, the feminine side of divinity. To say that does not imply that its place should be exactly equivalent to the masculine, but it definitely does have a place which has been neglected. I don't claim any full knowledge on this subject any more than anyone else can, but I do have my intuitions. As they coincide, more or less, with tradition, common sense and the book of nature, I believe them to be relatively free of prejudice and cultural conditioning.

The fundamental duality of existence (and existence as I hope to have made clear must be dual in order for it to be known) can be described as Spirit and Matter or God and Nature, Subject and Object, and in sundry other ways that are variations on this theme but which all boil down to something like Life and Appearance. In this duality the former is always, in practically every culture, masculine and the latter feminine. No doubt there are exceptions but they, as the saying goes, just prove the rule. Humanity has a basic intuition about this and it is correct.

Now, it is interesting that the two are complementary but

always it is natural to put one before the other. This is not just the way we are used to doing it. It is how it is. The masculine principle is always put first (in any complementary pair one must come first) even in Tantra where this dualism is most developed and described as Siva-Sakti. Does this mean that the first is the primary principle, Life/Spirit, and the second, Appearance/Matter, is that principle's complementary opposite which enables it to express itself which it has to do as a duality? Thus spirit and matter in manifestation are, in a sense, modes of Spirit since on the highest plane of reality, the one completely self-subsistent state of being, there is only God, and spirit and matter are still unsundered, not yet expressed. So you can say that the second comes out of the first as its complementary principle in manifestation and the way it knows itself as itself, but you could not reverse this statement and put it the other way round. If that is the case, it points to a twofold relationship between these two principles which may be why so many problems arise when looking for an understanding of how they should interact and their role vis à vis one another.

On the one hand, there is the complementarity. Where there is one, there necessarily is the other and each is incomplete without the other. One cannot exist without the other and they need each other to grow and become more. This divine duality is the case in all the created worlds and in every situation in which life is expressed. But, on the other hand, matter, the receptive element in God, is the vehicle for spirit when it moves out into self-expression and in that sense the masculine principle does precede the feminine, which is its opposite in manifestation and the worlds of duality. It is not just that in a state of unmanifest oneness neither exist or both are latent. If so, how would the externalising process ever get started? It is more that Divine Being, in revealing itself, becomes positive and negative though these words are slightly misleading because here the negative is not absence of anything but a real principle. We are, after all, talking about God in whom and for whom everything is real. Perhaps a better way of describing this primal duality would be as active or initiating (God, they say, is Pure Act) and creatively receptive. Both are fully real but one exists for the other to express itself. You might say that without the Mother (mater/matter/*maya*) the Father cannot create because it is only through her being, her substance and in her space that his idea can take form and manifest. She is the second part of the duality through which the One God manifests himself and without which would remain forever unexpressed.

This is undoubtedly a difficult concept, which is why we tend to seek refuge in a simpler scenario of either one alone being real or both being equally so. But neither of those ways of looking at the picture of masculine and feminine as they relate to the depths of existence is wholly satisfactory. The truth seems to be a mixture of the two: complementarity and hierarchy. Perhaps one way of picturing this is to see that the sexes (as cosmic principles, first and foremost) relate to each other in two ways. One, on a horizontal level in which the masculine is on the right and the feminine on the left, and two, on a vertical level, in which the masculine is above (Sky or Heaven) and the feminine is below (Earth). This image will certainly cause problems today but it was probably the intuitive understanding of the past, before our minds were fogged over by materialism and ideology and innocent, natural perceptions lost. It is also supported by the fact of the sun and the moon and the relationship between these two lights in the sky, which quite clearly correspond on a deep level to masculine and feminine polarities.

It cannot be denied that this relationship along the vertical axis, in which the masculine precedes (in ontological terms) the feminine, has sometimes been abused by men in the past, principally by taking it out of context and misapplying it on the horizontal level where it is not valid or not valid in the same way. But that does not mean it is incorrect. What it means is that spirit is the primary principle in creation and matter its expression in form, indeed its expression *as* form, but the two always go together to make a whole, though with the proviso that spirit must be seen as the active principle and matter the receptive, and with the additional understanding that the fact that the masculine hierarchically precedes the feminine as the active principle in creation does not make man superior to woman, individually or collectively, in this world. The two have equal value as expressions of God, after all, both are made in his image, but they also have their real roles which are not by any means the same, and in some ways may even seem to be unequal.

I want to try to imagine the beginning of all things. What happened when God created the universe? From within the eternal night (as we must conceive it) of unmanifest being comes God the Creator. Therefore the first thing is an act of Will, the will or desire to create. Now this cannot come from nothing so it means that God, as Creator, is already there. Existence is already present in non-existence or non-manifested existence. There must be a Creator before there is creation, so the Creator must be there in the darkness of non-manifestation and must precede anything else. The Creator is the acting, masculine principle, and this is the first of all things, present from before all things. But then "the Spirit of God moved on the face of the waters". In order to create, the Creator must have something in which and from which to create, something to give form to his idea. This is the waters which is the receptive or feminine aspect of God and which becomes light once it is impregnated by the Spirit of God. As I envisage it, God draws this forth or projects it from himself and the resulting feminine side is both the womb and substance of creation. For there to be anything there must be two things, both the masculine and feminine principles. Each needs the other in the creative process – as if we didn't know that! And, in terms of the created universe, each has always existed.

There is nothing without the two of them interacting. However, in terms of existence "prior" to creation, the masculine principle was the prime initiator, just as the Will of the Creator preceded Creation. The feminine lay dormant until acted upon by him.

Another way to look at this is to see the two cosmic principles as the absolute and the infinite and note how the former gives expression to the latter when it moves from being to becoming. Think of the absolute as a point and the infinite as the rays that stream forth from that point when it manifests itself. In this scenario the absolute masculine is pure actuality and the infinite feminine is pure potentiality. One can also envisage the masculine and feminine principles as giving and receiving or expanding and contracting. The two always go together as movements in a single process but the first is always the initiating or preceding stage. The second makes the movement of the first possible but the first is the instigating factor.

Everything in the universe, from particles to galaxies and including space itself, is created out of the feminine principle, the Mother as the divine substance of God. She is the source and matrix of all manifested form in heaven and earth. However, creation comes from the mind of God the Father. It is his idea that initiates the process and which takes form in the substance of her being according to parameters (laws) that he has set up. But note that we are talking about divine realities here, so the feminine aspect may be the receptive aspect but that does not mean she is without a will or mind or consciousness of her own. But she, like Mary, lovingly submits to the Will of the Father and allows his imaginative power to be expressed through her, also imbuing it with her quality. So God the Father thinks the Creation and his thought bears fruit in the body of the Mother, which lies in darkness until awoken by him.

The idea that the feminine principle in some way derives from the masculine is echoed in the account of Eve being formed from Adam's rib. It is also found in the story of Sophia or Wisdom, of whom it says in Proverbs chapter 8 that "The Lord created me the first of his works long ago, before all else was made. I was there when he set the heavens in place, when he marked out the horizon on the face of the deep". One can dismiss these stories as fairy tales or inventions designed to boost patriarchal power but I think they are mythologies, symbolical presentations of truth. The same truth is enacted in Mary's acceptance of her role as the Mother of God: that is, of God in form, the incarnate God. This involved humble submission to the Spirit of God (as Mary submits to God, matter should submit to spirit) and it played out on a lower level what happened right back at the very dawn of creation. Mary, by her submission to God, eventually ascends to become Queen of Heaven, and one need not take this literally to see that Mary was indeed the perfect representative of this divine archetype.

We have seen that God becomes two in order to express himself, but as the Creator he is the Father. This is why there is a sense in which the masculine does precede the feminine in terms of being even though there is full complementarity in the phenomenal worlds of becoming where the two are always ever present, each suggesting the other. Complementarity means that each has a role to play and neither should usurp the role of the other. That is not what is happening in our fallen world, but those who are serious about the spiritual path have to look within themselves and try to gain a proper intuitive understanding of the roles of the sexes and the meaning of sex as it exists at the deepest level of creation. Divine order only comes about when masculine and feminine are in harmony. In our human terms that does not mean that men are just manifestations of the masculine principle and women are just of the feminine. It's like the famous yin/yang symbol where each includes an element of the other. And, as human beings we all contain the whole within ourselves. Nevertheless, for women this should be in the context of femininity just as for men it should be within that of masculinity. At the moment, the world is confused, misled partly through the desire to correct past error but also, I would say, through envy and resentment stirred up and given spurious justification by demonic incitement.

All of which means that this discussion of the feminine aspect of divinity should not be taken as support for modern feminism. In fact, feminism, as it has become today, is often a misrepresentation of this idea since it is largely based on distaste for the feminine as the feminine and the desire to replace that with a pseudo-masculinity. Its devaluing of the role of motherhood is an indication of that. Its reluctance to see femininity in terms of receptivity, which it mistakenly sees as inferior, is another example that it has taken a wrong turning.

I have been talking here about principles but the question arises as to whether these principles are persons, too. I think the answer must be, yes, though what form they take, if form they have, is beyond our comprehension. In the Christian worldview, to which I largely adhere, everything in the universe is, or is aiming to become, a person based on the supreme reality that is the Personhood of God. Therefore all principles can be personified, but what that really means is open to question. Man is created in the image of God but we must try to conceive spiritual realities in spiritual rather than material or worldly terms. Is God a person? Yes. He is "I". "I am who I am", he says of himself. Does he have a body? Not according to Jesus who said that God is Spirit. Not according to St Paul who in Colossians 1:15 described Jesus as the image of the invisible God. And not according to the understanding that sees the Creator as transcending his creation and a being that cannot be limited by form. So not so much *a* being (though as Father he does have that aspect too) as Being in itself. I don't doubt that there are great spiritual beings who do appear in form and maybe the Divine Mother is one of them, as in the resplendent vision of Isis in *The Golden Ass* by Apuleius, but God as Creator of the Universe stands above his creation, notwithstanding the fact that he is fully immanent also.

It might be asked where the Trinity fits into this or the Godhead, the Divine Darkness beyond all being about which nothing can be said for before it all words must fade into silence. The latter can be equated with the Night of non-manifestation, before the Father creates. As for the Trinity, perhaps the Mother is the substance to its essence. Stratford Caldecott in his book *The Radiance of Being* gives us a clue when he says, "Creation takes place in the nothingness that is not "outside" but "within" God: that is, in the infinite spaciousness of the divine Trinity." Might it be the Mother who enables the Father to give expression to the Son and so allows the Logos to take form, both individually and cosmically? But really God is far too great and beyond our conception to be forced neatly into any ideas we might have about him. There may be different ways of conceiving him which are not contradictory but which focus on different aspects of the totality of what he is. This should not be a problem. We can look at the picture in different ways and this is one of them, but I see it as more a symbolic description of reality than an absolutely true depiction. Nevertheless, I believe that it does describe this reality in a way that does not misrepresent it on our level of understanding.

I have one more word to say on this subject. God, nowadays, is often described as transcending any idea of sexual distinction: either above masculine and feminine or else including both within himself. If we are positing a non-manifesting, inactive principle of spirit as pure is-ness, that would no doubt be correct. But if we are talking about the Creator, the one who created the universe, who created our souls and made us individual beings, the one whom Jesus Christ called Father and with whom we can have a relationship, then what I have written above applies. Naturally, the fact he is Father does not mean he doesn't contain all qualities and principles within himself, but still, as the Creator, he is Father. That doesn't mean he is biologically male but, as a Person, he is masculine and all souls are feminine to him which is made further clear from the fact that souls can only become spiritually alive through receiving spiritual impregnation, otherwise known as grace, from him.

Is reality ultimately personal or impersonal? If the latter, as with the god of the philosophers, it is difficult to see how the former could ever have arisen or how love, beauty and goodness could have the meaning they do. Ultimately they would be swallowed up, being just pointers to absolute oneness. And if they don't have any ultimate meaning, then they don't have true meaning at all. However, if reality is personal, as the Judeo-Christian revelation maintains, then life is actually alive and love is real and goodness is truth. I would maintain that the personal is not a lower, more relative, manifestation of the impersonal absolute but the very heart and point of existence. So the personal is not a limited or bound aspect of the impersonal, but the impersonal is simply a non-manifested aspect of the personal, and it is the personal that is true, ultimate reality. The foundation of the universe is not pure being but I AM.

And here, perhaps, we have clue to the whole mystery. God in the absolute sense is I AM so transcendent to any conjectural duality. But when he expresses himself in creation, the Creator then becomes the masculine polarity and creation is feminine to him. Thus, from pure Subject comes Subject and Object, and I believe this gives us an insight into the heart of the origin of the masculine/feminine polarity and a pointer as to what it really means.

For here, as Subject and Object, we have the two cosmic principles in their most undifferentiated forms. Now in the context of creation all human beings contain both principles within them so this is not a description of men and women. Reality is much subtler than that. Nevertheless it does point to an archetypal truth about the two sexes and is a guide as to the fundamental dynamics of the relationship between them.

Perhaps an image that best sums up the idea behind this chapter is that of a couple engaged in a dance such as the waltz, in which both partners are equal but the man leads. It would be nice to think that a profound truth is encapsulated in the symbolism of the dance.

Spirituality Without God

Can you have spirituality without God? I ask this question because for two thousand years people in the West would have replied, "Obviously not." The question would have seemed absurd, a complete contradiction in terms. Now, however, more and more people seem to think that you can, and maybe even should, for a spirituality without God is actually a higher thing than one with him. The idea of God is a limitation on pure consciousness runs the theory. I shall go into that in a moment. But first the question to ask is, why would anyone want a spirituality without God? Why would you not wish there to be a being of boundless love and wisdom behind all that is?

Part of the answer clearly lies in egotism and intellectual pride. This is a result of the fallen consciousness that will not submit and wishes to be God itself. It is the old *non serviam*. We want spirituality without God because we want complete autonomy, and that is the ego.

What about Buddhists, you say. They have no need of God. I actually think they do but I would also point out that Buddhism arose in a completely different culture to that of the modern, materialistic West. There was much less sense of individuality and much more theism of a largely ritualistic kind that had sunk into formality and dogma. In this context the philosophical insights of Buddhism were greatly enriching consciousness openers. They swept away superstitious cobwebs and introduced an abundance of useful spiritual practices to enable the human mind to transcend its psychological limitations. But Buddhism had its own limitations, and the absence of God was one of them.

For God is real. He is not an illusion or lesser reality. He is the Creator and you cannot reach real spiritual understanding without acknowledging this in some way. This is why both meditation and prayer are important. I am not saying that

Buddhism is a false religion, but I do see it as an incomplete one, and especially so for modern Westerners because it does not sufficiently take their core problem, which is a strong sense of self, into account. That may seem a decidedly odd thing to say since the essence of Buddhism is the denial of the reality of self. However, in practice, if people deny the existence of something intellectually, they make no real attempt to purify and ultimately sanctify it. I mean by this that if you theorise that self is an artificial construct which is basically unreal, you will not see the need to dedicate yourself to God and do his will, and that is the fundamental spiritual task and the only one that puts us in right relation with the universe and its maker, this being the relation of love. Not compassion, which is a human thing, but love which is divine.

"Remember the Creator" is one of the most important spiritual teachings there is. It is simple and to the point, and it is a teaching that Western Buddhists need to learn if they would find a true spiritual understanding and not remain locked in the ground base of their own being, failing to see that root consciousness is not God. That is perhaps less likely for those who follow the Mahayana form of Buddhism for there the sense of God has crept back in, in a certain way. However, even they need to open themselves up to the full reality of a Creator and personal God in order to become aware of the complete spectrum of spiritual reality and live the life that God intended for human beings, a life in which Creator and created have a full relationship based on love.

As for the belief that the entry into the pure consciousness of absolute being is a spiritual state that transcends any condition in which the sense of self remains, see the next chapter for a piece that expresses the opposite view. In brief, though, the idea is that God creates human beings and the whole world of becoming in order for life to grow and expand in love and creativity through the integration of being and becoming, the One and the Many, rather than the rejection of one for full focus on the other. After all, why does God create or, if you prefer, why is there something rather than nothing? If Nirvana were the goal and the personal just a stain on the pure whiteness of being, why would anything ever need to have come about? Indeed, how could it have done so unless a personal God was there from the beginning or, better put, before the beginning? The personal is not an illusion or lesser reality but the very point of life and expressed being. Yes, we must realise our oneness with God, but in that oneness there always remains the individual for relationship and the creativity that comes from that (not just entry into absolute being) is the purpose of our existence. And when you think about it, isn't it better that way? To believe this is not wish fulfilment but a response to a true and correct intuition within us. A response to what we are.

And those who think that ultimate reality must be pure oneness with no differentiation within it (as opposed to the three in oneness of the Trinity) should reflect on the fact that if it were, that's all it would ever be. There would not be the possibility of creation or even illusion.

The point I am making here is that any genuine spiritual awakening in the West should be theocentric and that Buddhist or non-dualistic type spirituality, popular amongst intellectuals drawn to some kind of spirituality because it doesn't conflict too much with modern scientific materialism, is insufficient. Let it be an introduction to higher truths but it must eventually be superseded by the full acknowledgement of God or a nascent spirituality may remain grounded or be side-tracked into a concern with self-realisation. What was right for the ancient East at a certain time is not right for the modern West except as an initial aid to turning away from materialism. Spiritual awakening can easily be derailed, and it will be unless it has God at its centre.

God Transcends Nirvana

I first became interested in Buddhism almost forty years ago but felt at the time that, despite its many insights, it ultimately fell short of the ideal as a description of spiritual reality. The intervening years have brought a greater understanding of the religion but my conclusions about it remain much the same. I feel that the Buddha found and articulated the highest state open to man unaided and on his own, which is the entry into pure being, for want of a better expression. But this is not the final destination intended for the human soul by its Creator though it may, if it wishes, rest there. But if it does, either through its own desire or through ignorance, it is accepting a secondary condition.

Buddhism does not acknowledge God which is its major failing. In every other respect it is a religion of great beauty and profound wisdom but that is a pretty big omission. Because it denies God (and it does do that because if it doesn't accept him then it denies him) it fails to see that the goal of the human soul is not to be absorbed into the Nirvana state of pure being but to be consciously made one with the Creator in a perfect union of the individual with the universal. Only in such a way can the whole of life, comprising being and becoming, the one and the many, spirit and matter and so on, be integrated and reconciled in a manner that does justice to all aspects of the created and uncreated realms. The purpose of our lives is not to forsake the reality in creation (which includes relationships with other beings) for pure consciousness, but to bring the two poles of existence together in a reunion that gives each one its due place in the hierarchical scheme of things. Only in this way can Man become a full co-creator with God which is his divine destiny.

Despite beliefs to the contrary, there are various kinds of mystical experience and attitudes to reality resulting from them but, for my purpose here, I would like to boil these down to the monistic and the theistic. The former is non-dualistic while the latter is dualistic, with the proviso that, properly understood, it is a dualism in which there is a complete underlying oneness, though one could just as well say that it is a oneness in which difference is also present, with the two being held in perfect equilibrium. Hence it combines and integrates the two. It has been said that monism is a higher realisation than theism, into which the latter is subsumed when a person realises his identity with the whole, having come to perceive that pure consciousness is all there is and the idea of an individual self is no more than a thought in the mind. Everything, the individual, the world, God, is just a manifestation of the One Life. This may seem to have a logical sense of progression to it but I think it is mistaken. What the monist does is attain to the unified ground of being through detachment from the "sheathes" that cover consciousness. He strips away all that is not consciousness and is left with the root of existence.

This is a true state of being, but is it what we were created for? Does it fulfil the totality of what we are? Could there be a higher state which combines the qualities of being and becoming to make something entirely new, something not possible in pure being alone? I believe there is and that it is union with God, a union in love with a, or, better put, the Person. The monist reaches the bedrock of existence but God is beyond this, containing but transcending it. It is his being but it is not his Person. The monist or non-dualist (there is a difference but it is mostly a technical one) assumes he has attained to the ultimate because there is nothing left to strip away, and he has reached perfect peace and unity of being. He feels he is the All and that it is him. However, he has sacrificed his God-given individuality in this quest and thereby missed the truth that undifferentiated oneness is a lower condition than union in love. For the higher goal than simple entry into pure being is the union of this existential oneness with the variety and capacity to grow of becoming. It is not the Absolute alone but the Absolute and the relative together. It is not pure spirit but the union of uncreated spirit and created soul. This is the extraordinary truth behind the reason for life in this world and the created order in general. It is why enlightenment or liberation (largely a matter of knowledge, whether that be direct perception or insight gained through meditation) must take second place in a hierarchy of spiritual understanding to a union with God which is only possible through love. Overcoming the ego through detachment and intellectual insight is one thing, and can theoretically take you to the uncreated core of yourself, which is identical with the uncreated core of all beings. But voluntarily offering up the self in love is another thing altogether, and points to the higher state of the sanctified soul in which individuality is not rejected, dismissed, seen as illusionary, denied or even transcended but made perfect in holiness. And this is only possible through the combined action of self-purification, love and grace.

The Buddha reached the highest state possible to unaided man, the ground and root of being. He attained complete detachment from all manifested forms of existence. He rejected desire and found a way beyond suffering, which was the initial motive behind his search. But though he penetrated to the depths of reality, he did not see that the ground of existence is not the same as God who includes this in himself but stands above it in his Person. It may be that the time had not yet arrived for this revelation and it had to wait for the advent of Christ to be made known. Christ, be it noted, did not try to escape suffering but accepted it, offering it up to the Father in loving sacrifice. In so doing, he showed the way to cleanse the self of its fallen will and thereby render it open to sanctification.

When I consider the teachings I received from my spiritual instructors I find that they support this view. There is a higher and more glorious destiny than Nirvana that awaits those who choose to follow it, and it is the union of the soul with its Maker. A union in which oneness and difference are both perfectly present, and one, moreover, capable of ever deeper development, unlike Nirvana which, if not static, cannot be considered open to change. My teachers did not spell this out since they didn't work like that. They guided but left me free to find things out for myself through my own endeavours. But the teachings they imparted point to it. Their insistence on love and humility as the primary qualities to be acquired by the disciple, along with their advice to **remember the Creator** and **be centred in God,** certainly indicate that.

Now, these instructions, on the face of it so simple as to be almost mundane, actually contain the essence of the spiritual path and, if followed faithfully, can take one to the highest goal. There is nothing quite like them in the teachings of the Buddha. But note that they must be followed with one's whole being to be properly effective, for you cannot be centred in God as long as you are identified with the lower or outer self. If you identify yourself exclusively with the "name and form" aspect of your being, your (in my case) William Wildblood self, you are not centred in God but in yourself whatever your spiritual feelings might be. Neither are you remembering the Creator, who might be in your thoughts as an image but will not be in your heart as a living presence. And this is where the teachings of Buddhism can be a great help for, if they do not in themselves lead to union with God, they can certainly bring the disciple to the point of complete detachment from the lower self, which is where you need to be in order to begin to be centred in God.

I realise that to say that Buddhism shows the way to the ground of existence but does not lead to God himself, who is a step further on, will be rejected by many. Nevertheless, I believe that God in himself goes beyond this ground or, at any rate, the ground as it exists in the human being, which may be identical with God's being but is not the totality of God in himself who remains transcendent as well as immanent. Non-dualists like to tell us that theism is dualistic and therefore on a lower level than their philosophy, but they do not appreciate that, while there certainly is a theism of straightforward duality, there is also one in which oneness and duality co-exist, and this is the one I am talking about here.

This is not the simplest of subjects to write about. How can there be something more than oneness? However, I hope to have said enough to trigger an intuitive response in anyone who feels that the non-duality teachings omit something important. It may be objected that I am saying that the Buddha was wrong and who am I to do that? But either he or Jesus was mistaken, since they are not, despite what many people claim nowadays, saying the same thing. I find the teachings of Christ not only more profound but more in keeping with reality, too. Non-dualists might claim that they do not deny duality but their position transcends it, viewing it as part of the relative world only. But the fact is that they misconceive the relative world, rejecting it as insignificant in the light of the Absolute and not realising that it fulfils the Absolute by giving expression to it. They have yet to appreciate that there is a higher duality beyond non-duality which encompasses oneness in the context of difference and vice versa. Moreover, I would like to ask how many non-dualists really love God, and how many just pay lip service to him as an idea, the need for which they have transcended and therefore are no longer required to concern themselves with. They should know that something is only transcended if it is fully experienced and its qualities absorbed. And no one transcends God.

Buddhism teaches the fact of absolute reality and outlines the way to it, but it neglects the all-important personal aspect and so it misses that the highest truth is not the disappearance of the individual into the universal but the integration of the individual with the universal. And this is why, while it advocates an impersonal compassion, it doesn't really know love in the full Christian sense, which has to be foreign to it since love requires the reality of the person. Mahayana Buddhism tries to make up for this deficit with its teachings on the Bodhisattva but it cannot really do so and acknowledge the reality of the person without betraying its fundamental principles, which means that the attempts to do so are never very satisfactory or coherent.

Buddhism and Christianity

According to Buddhism there is no "I". Our sense of self is an illusion based on faulty perception. An individual is no more than the combination of the five *skandhas* or aggregates of existence which can be summarised as 1) the physical form, 2) the emotions and sensations, 3) thinking and conceptualising, 4) habits, prejudices and will (grouped together as psychological formations), and 5) consciousness as reaction to the six external objects which are those associated with the five senses and the mind. These are regarded as empty, using the classic Buddhist term, in that there is nothing real (as in an individual) behind them. Rather, it is they that create that idea. Buddhism is not nihilistic because it says that there is a reality beyond this (that's the whole point of it, of course) but the individual has no part in this reality.

This is very good theory and sounds intellectually rigorous enough to be true but it is not true, certainly not the complete truth. Where our individuality is concerned, the whole is not just the sum of its parts. There *is* an individual soul and that is not an illusion. It was created so it cannot perhaps be said to be absolutely real, speaking in the very strictest of terms, but it is certainly not unreal. Ultimately there may only be God, or the Unborn, Unmade and Uncompounded, as Buddhists say, but existence is not made up of the absolute alone. It is a combination of the absolute and the relative or uncreated and created, and the two together make the whole. You cannot deny either one of them, even if you must see the relative as contingent so an aspect of the absolute and not real in its own right. Nevertheless, what God creates is real and cannot be denied. This is the crux of the matter.

What this means is the following. Out of the unmanifest darkness before time, God creates the manifest universe from his own being. Why? Hinduism calls this his play (*lila*), Islam says that God was an unknown treasure and desired to be known. I would say that the very nature of God is that he expresses himself in love, and this he does by creating free individuals who have their own intrinsic reality, given by him but none the less real for all that. But (and this is where the Buddhist position points to the truth) you as you are only relatively real in the sense that your goal is to outgrow identification with the limited, separate self and realise yourself to be one with the Universal Self or God. But that does not mean that the dewdrop slips into the shining sea and is now completely absorbed by the whole because, if it did, then what would be the point of creation? The restrictive identification with self is outgrown but self remains as, unless we are to disappear into nothingness and no longer be, it must. It is seen in an entirely different light and is no longer the centre of our being, which is now God, but it remains as our expressed self and the vehicle of our realisation. You might think of the God-centred soul as Janus-like in that it looks two ways. Inwards to the absolute, where there is no self or rather One Self, that is to say, only God, but outwards, too, where the individual still exists as a particular expression of the absolute, its focus on a unique point.

In the book *Towards the Mysteries* by Swami Omananda, the Masters make the following statement. **God made man Individual. Krishna was Individual. Muhammad was Individual. Christ was Individual.** As was the Buddha. This was the very reason and point of creation. One of the most repeated sayings of these Masters was that we should **be individual without being individualistic**. The Masters who spoke to me had the most wonderful individualities but they were not identified with those. They lived and moved and had their being in what they would sometimes call the Most High. Paradoxically, they were more fully individual than anyone I have ever met, and it occurs to me that it is only when we have transcended our limited focus on the separate self that we can be a true individual. We need to go beyond the individual and not be bound to it, Buddhism is right there, but individuality is not an illusion. It is, in fact, the basis of love, and love is at the heart of creation.

I have no desire to get caught up in theorising about the nature of ultimate reality, but I do think it important to get at the truth as far as we can because that will affect our approach to reality, and this is why I reject the Buddhist doctrine that self is an illusion. At its best, this doctrine can be considered as a technique or "skillful means" to help the disciple give up his exclusive identification with his ego-bound, phenomenal self but it should not be taken literally. For there is a real individual self beyond the purely phenomenal version of it.

All of which leads to my belief that there is confusion in Buddhism between the ego and the individual. The ego is an illusion, if you want to use that word, born of identification with the mind. It is our creation. But the individual soul is the creation of God. God multiplied himself to become more, to grow and expand and increase his delight. This was why he created. Yes, in absolute terms we may come to realise our fundamental being as identical with the primordial state, but the human being is not just spirit. It is spirit, soul and body (reflecting the Trinity) and all of these have their place in the whole. It is that which gives life its variety and richness. It is that which reflects the reality of love. To cut off and deny parts of the totality of what you are in an attempt to find the truth is not a good idea. You may well find a centre of peace and oneness but you will lose something important. There is certainly a hierarchy of being and it should be seen from above downwards, but all levels have their place in the hierarchy and none are illusionary or to be discarded in the search for an ultimate reality. Not if you wish that search to end successfully.

If there is no self then who attains Nirvana? You might say that the realisation of the non-existence of the self is Nirvana but then you also have to ask what realises this non-existence. Again, you might say it is the Self realising the Self but the Self knows itself eternally anyway. In terms of *this* realisation, it is a specific individual that has realised its oneness with the universal Self, and that individual is now, for the first time, truly undivided which, after all, is what individual actually means.

We are made in the image of God. God has individuality and so do we, given by him without reservation for the fulfilment of love.

This is a statement which could not be made by a Buddhist. It is a Christian statement, and it points to the fact that there is a profound spiritual disagreement between the two religions. Try as we might, we cannot pretend that they are saying the same thing. Many people do try and Christianity is often regarded by the mystically inclined as though it is saying the same thing, really, as Buddhism. It just isn't saying it quite as well. I disagree. The writings of some Christian mystics can be interpreted as if they are speaking non-dualistically, though Meister Eckhart is usually the only one who can really be seen in this light, and then only if one reads him selectively. But non-duality or monism, as conceived in Eastern terms, is not part of Christianity at all which remains a dualistic religion, in that union with God and not absolute identity, is the goal. Faced with this problem I have tried to understand how Buddhism and Christianity, both seemingly true on their own terms but incorrect in terms of each other, stand in the light of overall truth, and the conclusion I have come to is that Buddhism is the highest truth but Christianity is higher.

Before I try to explain that rather gnomic utterance, I should say that this view is fully borne out by the teachings the Masters gave me. They never mentioned either Buddhism or Christianity by name, though they did speak of Jesus, but what they taught can be seen to contain elements of both, the essential elements required for any individual treading the spiritual path, though tailored for my particular needs of the time. For instance, they spoke of both meditation and prayer as being equally important. They told me to **forget the personal self and merge with the universal Self** but also said I should **remember the Creator**. They spoke of themselves as being essentially one but were also wholly individual. They advocated detachment from emotional identification but, above all, they emphasised love and humility as the highest spiritual qualities, neither one of which would have any meaning in a system of pure non-duality. How could they? Both pre-suppose the reality of the individual.

I say Buddhism is the highest truth because it points to the unchanging reality beyond creation and the movement of form, and details the way in which an individual may step out of the world of becoming and into pure being. This is Nirvana, the "blown out" state in which there is no more coming and going. Oneness with the Absolute must be the highest state. It is the state beyond all ideas of states.

Or so it might seem. But actually, there is something more, something better, and this is revealed in Christ.

For in Christ, the world of creation, either denied outright or diminished in Buddhism and other non-dualistic philosophies, is fulfilled. He is the fulcrum of the created world and uncreated reality, and in himself he reveals the perfect union of the two. He brings the one to perfection and the other to full expression and, as a result, completes them both. For while Buddhism rejects becoming for being, Christ encompasses the whole of life in himself and shows us the way to do the same, which way is through and by means of his teachings and his person.

For the Buddha the problem of life was resolved through the elimination of suffering but this also required the elimination of desire. The way of Christ is more inclusive. It involves, not the elimination of desire and suffering, but their redemption and sanctification. This is the higher path that leads to the fullest embracing of life, and not the rejection of any natural part of it. You could say that Buddhism and similar philosophies reject matter for spirit, but in Christ, matter and spirit are made one in a holy union in which the former is sanctified and the later revealed. And from this union is born something completely new, something in which the divine qualities of goodness, beauty and truth are not transcended and left behind as belonging to the relative world, as they must necessarily be in a strict non-duality, but taken up and transformed and carried along on a journey that progresses into ever deeper union and ever brighter illumination. Nirvana is an end. There is nothing more. There can be nothing more. But the way shown by Christ has no end for in it time is taken up into eternity and something more than either one on its own comes into being.

Buddhism appeals to the modern intellectual who is looking for some form of deeper understanding in the spiritual wasteland of the 20th and 21st centuries, but it can be a risky spiritual approach for Westerners. It falls too neatly into our modern ways of thinking, and can be adjusted to suit our current prejudices. Its lack of a personal God is a temptation to intellectual pride.

That is one reason I regard Buddhism as an unsuitable path for the contemporary Westerner. The fact that it appears to offer spirituality without the inconvenience of God makes it attractive to some but that is its major flaw in my opinion and why, whatever its historical necessity and appropriateness in its original time and place, it is not really appropriate for Western people. The cultural context is quite different, and it tends to fortify existing deficiencies rather than correcting them as it would have done in the heavily theistic and ritualistic context in which it arose. Even in India it needed correction, which is why we had first Sankara and then Ramanuja who offered a more inclusive teaching than did his predecessor, one which reconciled unity, God and the individual.

But for us today, Buddhism or any spiritual approach which doesn't acknowledge the Creator, coincides too readily with our assumptions about life and can be too easily fitted in with our materialism. But our assumptions need to be disturbed not flattered. The Buddha did that to the people of his time but we are totally different from them, and need an approach which challenges and confronts our worldly prejudices. As I see it, the great danger in not acknowledging a Creator is that our spirituality is human-centric, which means that potentially we will remain in the fallen state in which the self is dominant. I know that Buddhism has the express aim of revealing the emptiness of the self but that just will not work for modern Western people for whom the self is so entrenched that it can never be bypassed if, indeed, it can for anyone at any time. It must be first purified and then transformed by grace, and the best way to do this remains the way shown by Jesus whose arrival in this world changed everything, rendering other approaches secondary, even if they remain effective on their own terms, as indeed Buddhism does. Faithfully followed, it may take its most developed practitioners to enlightenment. But Christ offers something better than this, more in line with God's purpose for his children. He offers the spiritual transformation of self rather than its elimination, and it is this that fulfils the reason for creation and incorporates all its goods rather than rejecting any of them.

If we accept that human beings are made of spirit, soul and body, then we see that Buddhism and similar approaches reject the last two for more or less exclusive focus on the first. Modern practitioners may claim they don't do this but in effect they do, or should if they are true to the teachings. The no self doctrine is clearest proof of that. Christianity, on the other hand, sees a human being equally as spirit, soul and body or inner life, intrinsic quality and outer appearance, and gives all of these their due importance. They all have their place in an overall scheme of things, even if the priorities are always from above downwards. Thus, in Christianity, the individual self is not lost as it is in non-dualistic religions, or even seen as belonging to a lesser reality. It is sanctified by grace and taken up to the highest reality. It is not seen as the centre of consciousness any longer, that is God, but it remains the truth of what a person is, even in its transformed state once the soul has become one with spirit.

When Christ ascended into heaven his body ascended also, foreshadowing what will happen to the whole of creation at the end of time. This was the most profound act there could be, demonstrating, as it did, the perfect union of spirit and matter, the latter wholly obedient to the former. It is our destiny if we will accept it.

Man is Made in the Image Of God

A core message of this book is that God is personal and not the impersonal absolute of many forms of mysticism, particularly Eastern, but increasingly Western, too. So rather than the undifferentiated oneness that these approaches to truth offer, it is the combination of oneness and individuality that is the highest state open to Man, and the reason for this world of creation in which everything has a value and nothing is illusion except the darkness of separative existence. Though even this can become a perceived reality for us if we go too far in its direction. Perhaps that is what hell is.

God is a Person – capitalised because he is the source of all personhood, our possibility of being a person deriving from the reality of him as Person. Do you not feel a sense of relief in hearing that? It means that you are loved, and that there is a purpose behind everything that happens in this world. We are too quick to dismiss this idea as anthropomorphic and say that we have made God in our own image. That may be true for many of the pagan gods, though these may also be created beings of some kind, but it is not true of the one living God and Creator who is the source and pattern of all the highest and best in us: of truth, love, beauty, goodness, and of the capacity to give and to sacrifice without thought of reward. Everyone feels these qualities within themselves to some degree, however overlaid by greed, ignorance and selfishness they might be, and everyone recognises that they are laudable and should be encouraged, unless they are sunk so low in self-hatred and bitterness that they cannot rise above cynicism or pride. They are the stamp of the divine Person within us, the reflection of his qualities and, however dim and imperfect that reflection may be, it is still the image of God shining in our hearts, and we can always use it to connect ourselves to our Creator.

God is not like us. We are like him, though only so in terms of our best and truest selves. If he had intended us to rest in pure consciousness beyond form, which is the non-dualist goal, there would have been no need to undergo the experience of life in this world. No need to develop a sense of values, of courage and the ability to endure suffering cheerfully. But there is the need to learn these things because they make us actively good rather than just neutral or detached, and that is why we are here. It is why God conceals himself from us and why we live in a world of opposites where evil and suffering are not only possible but likely, indeed inevitable. It is only through struggle that we rise and are able to bring out the potential that exists within us.

So, far from desiring us to deny our individuality, God wants us to develop it from the seed he has implanted within us. He does not want clones. He wants free individuals, but ones who are individual not individualistic. The difference is all important. Know that there is no contradiction between oneness and individuality. This is simply how things are in a universe in which the One is the underlying reality but the many is the expressed reality, and the reason for that is that God, the fundamental "I AM", finds the greatest joy in always becoming more. It is his nature to give and to expand (through us) and to know both the bliss of being and the joy of becoming, which latter is also the means and fulfilment of his primary quality of love. Those who think of the absolute as beyond and above all qualities have misconceived the nature of God and creation. It might seem a reasonable assumption, and yet the highest truth is not in pure being alone but in bringing being and becoming into a sweet harmony, with each completing the other. Isn't a beautiful painting better than a blank canvas? Pure unbroken oneness would mean that love was an illusion, but love is the essence of existence because God is not just one but three in one, a deep mystery and yet plainly reflected in nature, whether that be concretely in Man, Woman and Child or abstractly in subject, object and the relationship between them.

Divine reality has been perceived by human beings in this world as sometimes impersonal and sometimes personal. Over the last 100 years or so it has become more common to think that the former conception is nearer the truth. But this is a mistake, caused by our current intellectual focus as well as a rejection of earlier, possibly simplistic ideas about a personal God. It is more accurate to say that God is personal in his true self-nature but includes an impersonal aspect as the one life which exists throughout creation. It is him as immanence. We can identify with this life aspect, if that is our wish, but it is a less comprehensive state than that of union with God. And note that the impersonal compassion of Buddhism is a lesser thing than the joy of divine love known in union and when creation is embraced as fully real, as the expression of its Maker: not regarded simply as a lesser state of illusion or dream that is dissipated in the light of the Absolute.

Oneness underlies the multiplicity of expressed reality but it is not the whole story. It does not make creation insignificant since creation comes about specifically to make something more than simple oneness. An impersonal absolute could never create. It would just be itself. Creation needs a mind and a mind means a person. There is no getting away from this. God is personal, and that means our individuality is real. We do not "go beyond" it. We do go beyond exclusive identification with it, but we retain our unique quality and, if we did not, what would become of love which needs an object, of beauty which needs a form and of goodness which must be expressed? They would be nothing. The aspect of pure being in the divine nature is not all there is to God, and nor is it all we are. Man is spirit, soul and body, manifesting as our life, our quality and our form. These are all fundamental aspects of the totality of what we are and can't be separated. Like our Creator, in whose image we are made, we are three in one.

I was once asked a question on this subject which went something like this.

"Esoteric metaphysics postulates a system in which Beyond-Being is the Absolute or impersonal Divine Essence, and the Personal God only exists at the level of Being which is called the first self-determination of the Absolute. So the Personal God is at a lower and more relative level of reality. This seems to correspond to the Kabbalistic Tree of Life with Ain Soph or absolute Nothingness manifesting as Kether, the first cause and root of Creation. In both of these systems God, as such, is a step down from the Absolute, and a mystical union with God would be a lesser realisation than Nirvana, which is entry into Beyond-Being or Ain Soph. This has a certain logical sense of progression to it but it seems you are saying something different."

This was my response.

I am saying something different. The difference is slight but significant. In the past I have thought in a similar way to the approach you describe, and believed that Nirvana must be a deeper realisation than the mystic's sense of oneness with God, for in that there is still duality present, me and God. That seems a logical way of seeing things. Union is trumped by non-duality which must be better than duality. But there was always a nagging doubt. If Ultimate Reality really is the formless Absolute, whence comes anything at all? Where does the Creator God come from? Why should Beyond-Being ever give rise to Being, unless Being is already present within it in some way, and if it is then that is duality. There is not just an absolute undifferentiated oneness. There is oneness and the potential, at least, for something else, something more. If Nirguna Brahman (Brahman without attributes) is the bedrock of everything, where do the qualities and attributes come from? How could they ever arise? So Saguna Brahman (Brahman with attributes) must be present in some way in Nirguna Brahman, which means that the Void, so called, cannot be completely empty, the Self cannot be pure consciousness alone, and the Absolute must already contain the Relative within it. There can be no such thing as pure being without the innate capacity to become always and fully present within it.

This is why I now don't go along with the idea that absolute reality is simply the divine darkness of no-thingness which is what Beyond-Being or Ain Soph or Nirvana would be. It's why I would no longer put the personal God on a lower level of reality than that state, seeing them now as simply two faces of the one reality, just the Absolute in different modes, relating to passive and active existence or rest and expression. But then even God at rest contains the active God, the Creator God, in itself. The Creator is not a limited mode of the Absolute but the Absolute in movement, in becoming mode. But this becoming is the expression of being, integral to it and not in any way a lesser reality. How can it be since to be at all, it must be there from the very beginning, indeed before the very beginning? Likewise, time must exist in eternity in order to exist at all, ever. We can say it only exists in theory or potential, but exist it must. It is not simply not there at all until suddenly it is. And so, if God is the Absolute in expression, which he is, then he is fully there already in the Absolute. He is not a lesser or more relative thing at all, which he would be according to the system you describe. He is not, and can never be, part of *maya,* as he is in a strict, non-dualistic system.

All this has implications for the question of individuality, denied in Buddhism and Advaita which don't properly appreciate the reality of the relative world. Individuality is a real, God-given thing, not an illusion of ignorance. And this means that a real enlightenment would not mean the end of the individual but the end of a limited identification with individuality which is a wholly different affair. The point of it is not the entry into changeless being or Nirvana but the conscious integration of spirit and soul to create something more than either on its own, which encompasses and involves the whole being, not just a part of it. This is found in the proper union of the soul with God, a union that accepts the totality of existence and does not seek to escape matter for spirit. It is the cosmic marriage that joins the two together, something that would not be possible if the root of reality really were the featureless Beyond-Being you describe. To say that Being comes from Beyond-Being can only be acceptable if we acknowledge that it is already wholly present in Beyond-Being, and is not a limited step down into a lesser reality.

For what is ignored by those who don't properly distinguish between God and the soul, because they think that both arise from and sink back into the Absolute of Beyond-Being, is that the ground of pure consciousness is not God. Self-emptying can take one to this ground, and it may then seem as though one has penetrated to the deepest mysteries because all has been stripped and there is nothing left but naked existence. But this is not God, or not the completeness of God. It is but an aspect of his being as existent in the soul. It is not his heart. The true mystic seeks a union of love with the heart of God. Heart to heart. This may be duality but it is a duality that has built on non-duality and is the real goal of creation which has to do with making something out of nothing. Who would be satisfied with changeless being instead of eternal love?

For the truth the non-dualists don't see is that identification with the ground is but a precursor to a loving relationship with the Creator. Because they make the mistake of envisaging formless being as beyond God, and see him as emerging from that, they confuse entry into the depths of their own soul with the spiritual goal. This is why some of them will say there is no path, no goal and all you have to do is to realise what you already are. But that is wrong. There *is* a path, there *is* a goal and it requires more to reach that goal than simply to know yourself as pure consciousness. That may take you to the core of your being but the mystic's goal of a union in love with God fulfils the purpose of creation in a way this does not because it unifies the two poles of life whilst fully preserving the integrity of them both. It does not deny love or the individual but sees these as the actual reason for creation. God created so that there might be a ceaseless expansion of light, and this there can only be when the one and the many are both fully valued. If one is rejected for the other, you are spiritually impoverished.

The conclusion we must draw is that twoness is actually a higher thing than oneness, metaphysically considered, as long as we understand it to include oneness as a base. Besides which, unqualified oneness cannot actually exist since for anything ever to have come about there must be a principle of differentiation right at the very heart of reality. Another way of putting this is to say that eternity must be dynamic if it is ever to be capable of expression.

From what I have written here and in earlier chapters it might seem that I reject the Buddhist approach to truth, but that is not the case. Its great value is that it takes the subject away from identification with himself and leads him to a deeper insight into the true inner nature of the human being. It gives an understanding of immanence that is lacking in most modern Christianity. At the same time, Buddhism and similar paths lack a proper awareness of the Creator and Father of the universe and so overlook the need to form a loving relationship with God. Hence it is incomplete and needs to be balanced by the Christian way, but then the same might be said in reverse, too. And so I return to the idea that both meditation and prayer are important for a complete approach to God, one that takes into account both his immanent and his transcendent aspects.

The Advaita Illusion

Buddhism is not the only philosophy to have influenced modern Western spirituality. I have mentioned another briefly in passing but in this chapter I would like to look at it a little more closely. By the way, I should say that I regard both influences as positive because they develop aspects of the whole that have not been emphasised so much in Christianity. I think Christianity holds the greater truth but it does not have a monopoly on truth, and it can be helpful to explore other approaches, though it is not essential.

The Advaita Vedanta of India is regarded by some people as the *ne plus ultra* of religion and metaphysics, the spiritual philosophy to which all others tend and for which they are only preparatory. This is because it uncompromisingly boils everything down to the One. Consciousness is not regarded as a property of the Absolute but its very nature. It is all there is and everything else, the world, the soul, even God, is reduced to an ultimately unreal manifestation of that. To its enthusiasts this idea seems a logical progression from the initial sense of multiplicity, and its radical purity and simplicity no doubt increase its attraction. At one time I assumed it was a legitimate approach to truth and that it was just another, albeit slightly extreme, philosophy that identified Man's origin and end as in God. But that was before I examined it properly and realised that its denial of self did not just mean that an exclusive identification with self had to be transcended by the spiritual person, but that self did not even truly exist in the first place. I now believe that Advaita is based on a one-sided misinterpretation of reality and a desire to force all experience into a pre-determined box. There is no doubt that its position has some metaphysical justification, but it leaves too much out to be accepted unreservedly, and, in the final analysis, it must be considered a reductive view of how things are.

Perhaps the first thing to appreciate when trying to understand Advaita is that it came out of its main proselytiser Sankara's attempt to save Hinduism from the increasing spread in India of Buddhism. So rather than a natural thing in itself, arising out of pure, spontaneous insight, it is better thought of as developing in reaction to something. It might even be considered, in part at least, as a compromise, and, indeed, later thinkers did accuse Advaitins of giving up too much in their efforts to rescue the religion of the Vedas and the Upanishads from the onslaught of Buddhism with its perceived atheism. Specifically, what they gave up was the idea of God and the reality of individual souls. This may seem academic in terms of attaining to an absolute consciousness but actually a proper understanding of the true metaphysical nature of things is all-important for determining correct spiritual practice.

Advaita is often perceived in the West as the essence of Hinduism and the point up to which the entire religion leads, but that is not in fact the case. There are competing points of view within Vedanta itself (Vedanta being the religion based on the Vedic scriptures) in particular that of Ramanuja who, while affirming fundamental unity, also taught the reality of individual souls, thereby rejecting Sankara's interpretation (and it was an interpretation) of the Upanishads. And then there is the non-Vedic Tantra which describes existence as Siva-Sakti, which roughly translates as Consciousness-Energy, and so confirms the reality of the two poles of existence which are different but not separate, and which need uniting or integrating in the disciple for enlightenment to take place.

Advaita, like Buddhism, reduces the individual to the ego or separate self, but there are no valid grounds for assuming that the self-reflective principle in a human being amounts to nothing more than a veil on pure, unlimited consciousness, and is, therefore, an illusion of ignorance. Just because the soul can transcend identification with itself and know its uncreated origin in God does not mean it does not exist. It is a failure of imagination on the part of non-dualists not to see that the individual can co-exist with the universal. Indeed, that these two should co-exist is the whole point of creation, as I hope to have made clear in previous pages. Of course, Advaitins do not believe in creation as such, seeing the world as little more than an illusion caused by ignorance of the real nature of things, but then they have no explanation as to why there should be something rather than nothing in the first place.

It is important to differentiate between ontological identity, which is above the world of sense-perception, and the notion of a separate self. That is to say, between the individual and unique "I" on the one hand, and the sense of "me, my and mine" on the other. Neither Advaita nor Buddhism do this, and part of the reason they fail to discriminate between the individual soul and the ego, its separated component, is that they have no understanding of the Fall as taught in Judeo-Christian religion. The closest they come to it is the Buddhist view that all life is suffering. So they see the self as inherently bad instead of understanding that it has gone bad, or been corrupted, but can be redeemed, a perfect example of throwing the baby out with the bath water. Or, perhaps more pertinently, rejecting the whole grain just because of the husk.

It might be countered to the above remarks that many non-dualistic teachers have obviously had some experience which proves to them the truth of their doctrine, and any intellectual arguments against it are irrelevant in the face of this higher knowledge. Granted, they may no doubt have experienced some kind of mystical at-one-ment. This is not that uncommon. In the great majority of cases it will be a contact with the soul which is the spiritual level of consciousness existing above the passing movement of time and the phenomenal world. However, this is then interpreted according to the pre-existing mind-set of the experiencer, and often in the context of Advaita or Zen or some similar belief system which seems to offer ultimate truth. To an up-until-now worldly mind any contact with the spiritual soul can seem so extraordinary that it might see it as obliterating the self, despite the fact that there has only been a temporary melting of the boundaries of the ego. But what matters with an experience is how you react to it, what you do with it, and to treat it as a reason to deny God and the individual self is to misinterpret it and could well arrest any further future spiritual development. In effect, the supposedly denied and non-existent ego is taking the experience to itself, adapting itself to the experience and possibly even subtly strengthening itself in the process, which is why false interpretations of spiritual states must be corrected. The disciple may end up worse off than when he started, spiritually speaking.

It is well known that Hindu mystics have visions of Krishna while Christian ones may see Jesus, and that in many cases this is because their already existing beliefs colour or even determine their experience. Similarly, a non-dualistic belief system will influence the subject's interpretation of his experience which assumes the form his mind imposes on it. That is why wise spiritual teachers do not recommend taking personal experience as the sole basis for comprehending reality. The imperfect nature of the mind receiving the experience is a factor in how it is understood. This is not a rejection of mystical experiences, but points to the truth that an experience and its interpretation are not the same thing.

At first sight Advaita might seem to teach a pure form of the standard mystical idea of union between man and God, but because it denies the full reality of both the individual soul and God it can lead to a mistaken idea of what spirituality actually is, and this will affect proper practice. Its absorption of everything into the One might make it seem the highest form of spirituality, and the one that lies behind all others as their uniting principle, and that is how it has been presented. And yet it is essentially reductive since it takes no account of any relationship between God and the soul, has no awareness of why the world should have come about in the first place, no real understanding of the many different levels of being and no insight into the fact that the soul is not just the ego.

To misconceive the nature of spiritual reality means that your approach to it might be completely wrong. The doctrine of Advaita has gained considerable intellectual respectability over the last hundred years, but it did not go unchallenged in the past in the land of its birth and should not go unchallenged now that it has become popular elsewhere. It seeks to express the most profound of truths but leaves out something essential, which is the reality of creation. I am not disputing that Man is ultimately woven of the same cloth as God and that we can know this in the sense of wholly realise it, but I reject the notion that individuality is an illusion to be seen through. If that is the case then love is also an illusion. I don't mean this entirely seriously but does the married non-dualist love his wife as a person or as a manifestation of Brahman, one amongst countless others? Tell her that on your next anniversary. Of course, if he is true to his doctrine he will not have a wife or, indeed, any kind of personal relationship at all.

I would also suggest that the non-dualist reduction of God to "the last thought", as I believe the Indian mystic Ramana Maharishi phrased it, is a category error. How can you limit God in this way? The Creator of form is clearly beyond form. How can God be restricted to thought on any level? I understand that Ramana refers to the conception of God not God himself, but then God is not limited to a conception of him. He is transcendent as well as immanent as well expressed by Krishna in the Bhagavad Gita, "Having pervaded this whole universe with a fragment of myself, I remain".

Now I have mentioned Ramana, I should address the fact

that his espousal of Advaita might make it seem unassailable. He is, after all, one of the major spiritual figures of the last century, and one about whom nothing but good has ever been said. However, two things about him should be borne in mind. First of all, his spiritual awakening was not attained within the context of Advaita, which he subsequently adopted as the one mystical system available to him that could be said to correspond to his experience. He used Advaita as the best framework to give form to his insight. I mean no disrespect to someone whose level of spiritual attainment was clearly very high to say that his experience of the world, both intellectual and actual, was not particularly extensive, and even the best of us must operate within the constraints of our environment, mental and physical. Ramana was a product of his world, as we all are, and had perforce to express himself within the limitations of that world. We would say that about Christian mystics of the order of St Francis of Assisi so why not about Ramana, too? So, although he is taken as a sage epitomising the truth of Advaita, it must be recognised that he did not come to his realisation through that path, and his utilisation of it was, to a large extent, part of his cultural heritage.

My reflections here are not made in a negative, critical spirit because there are things about Advaita that I admire. Its seeing beyond form to the pure reality of Brahman that lies behind all things is a great insight, albeit fully present in the Upanishads. However, by dismissing creation as *maya* and seeing created beings as having no reality other than an ephemeral, fundamentally illusionary one, it fails to admit a vital truth and it does this because it prioritises knowledge over love, which is a major spiritual error. Love is the keynote of the universe and it alone is capable of perceiving the highest truth. When the Masters told me **to forget the personal self and merge with the universal self**, they were not saying that the "I" they were counselling to do this had no existence, but that it had to go beyond itself. When they told me to see all beings as manifestations of the divine, they were not saying that these beings had no reality in themselves, but that God was present in everyone.

If I had to sum up what was missing in Advaita and other non-dualistic systems, I would say that reality encompasses both unity and multiplicity, and if you restrict it to one or the other then you have missed the mark. And this is what I think Advaita does. That does not mean it cannot be a valid spiritual path, but only up to a point. For it has limitations which should be understood. So when I say Advaita is illusion, I am not referring to its point that all things are manifestations of Brahman and that what that is, we, in our essence, are, too. But I do not accept its idea that the oneness of all things negates the reality of created things. For God created the world and everything in it, principally us, as an expression of his love. And when he created the world he saw that it was good. Therefore, Advaitins need to understand that the real perfection of being is not in oneness but in relationship. When Christ was crucified, he was not just seeing through the illusion of self but offering up his self in loving acceptance of his Father's will, and that is a far higher and more noble thing.

Non-Duality and the Person

One of the consequences of the seemingly unstoppable spread of the contemporary cult of atheism is that when people react against it and decide to follow a spiritual path, they often take a lot of their atheism with them. I mean by this that their atheistic assumptions have sunk so deeply into their minds that they don't see them for what they are. This can manifest itself in various ways but one of the most common seems to be that such people look for a spirituality without God. For some this might be seen as a purely intellectual choice, but for others it is a matter of wanting to drink the wine without thanking the host who provides it. The one who, in fact, made it.

Many Westerners who take to Eastern forms of religion are attracted to the non-dualistic varieties, either Buddhism, in which God plays no part at all or Advaita Vedanta, the philosophy of Sankara in which a God of sorts exists but plays no real part and who is eventually left behind as no longer relevant. The common point of both these is that the individual self is regarded as having no real existence. What you are is pure consciousness. In reality there is only the Absolute, and your aim is to know yourself as that. This view may appear to have a certain logic going for it but is it true? It's a powerful idea but, if not completely wrong, it certainly misses something vital because, while there may be a state of pure consciousness that a human being can enter into, you, as an individual, are also real and this turns out to be the greater truth. For God created you as an individual with whom he might have a relationship, and who might progress to ever-higher states of divine being, even becoming a co-creator with God. You may renounce that but, if you do, you are giving up life's richest reward.

Before I looked at Advaita seriously, I assumed it was just a more radical form of the basic spiritual philosophy that man and

God are ultimately one. Closer investigation, however, revealed unqualified non-dualism to be based on Sankara's rather selective cherry-picking of the Upanishads, interpreted in the light of Buddhism which he wished to contest but was obviously very influenced by. I now regard Advaita as tending to the reductive for it fails to see that the One and the Many are both essential in a universe in which the highest truth is in growth and relationship rather than static being. That is why it has no explanation for this whole world of creation: why anything came about in the first place and why there is this ignorance it believes to be the veil on reality.

We examined that in the last chapter but let me expand on it a little more here. Advaita is reductive because it denies the reality in creation, reducing life to the absolute alone, when in fact it is the absolute and the relative together, the eternal and created worlds moving and working together, with the union of the two bringing about something completely new. Sankara was a great philosopher but he was also a logician who couldn't deal with the apparently paradoxical statements in the Upanishads, so left out what didn't suit his thesis. For him the One and the Many must be opposites and only one of them could be true. This is why he has no explanation for creation, which he says is a mystery not to be understood. He can't see that it is God expressing himself in order to become more by creating other beings with whom he can have a relationship of love, and who can then contribute to creation themselves.

Some Advaitins claim that their philosophy does not dismiss creation or the individual as such, seeing them instead as "neither real nor unreal", but frankly this is just a piece of wordplay bordering on sophistry. At the end of the day, Advaita allows God and the soul a reality only on the level of ignorance. Fundamentally, it sees all difference and plurality as illusory. This may be interpreted to mean illusory in an ultimate sense, but either the individual is real or it's not. You can't have it both ways, and yet this seems to be precisely what Advaita tries to do when it takes the "neither real nor unreal" position. It wants to have its cake and eat it too, but the fact remains that, when you come down to it, there is no room for a true individuality in Advaita. The person, whether human or divine, is the product of ignorance.

This is why I regard Advaita as a one-sided view of reality that breaks down under proper scrutiny as it ignores the fact that what God creates is real and has a purpose. No doubt everything is one in essence but the individual is also real, and if that were not the case then love would be a fantasy. To give it reality only in the relative world of multiplicity, as Advaita is forced to do if it thinks of it at all, is little different to dismissing it altogether. But anyway, the point is that love is not only real in the relative world, it exists at the deepest level of being. You might even say that love *is* the deepest level of being. This could not be the case if the deepest level were pure unqualified oneness. Only the Trinity can account for love as a fundamental truth.

And this is where the Christian revelation goes further than any other religious teaching or metaphysical philosophy. Ultimate reality is not the oneness of complete unity, as it is for the Buddha or for Plotinus. It is the three in oneness of the Trinity. So it is more like a ceaseless dance of self-communion than unqualified abstract being, a continuous giving and receiving in love. This is such a remarkable truth that it makes the heart leap with joy to know it, which would seem to be a further confirmation of its authenticity. For it means that life is not static but able to grow and expand, in all probability limitlessly. It also explains the personhood of God and tells us that this is intrinsic to reality. However, the naturalistic legacy of atheism means that many modern spiritual seekers reject it, and take to the more scientific seeming philosophies of the East. Of course, there are branches of Hinduism which believe in a personal God but these are generally regarded as second tier as, in the context in which they arose, a kind of modified polytheism, they usually are.

So the mistake many people interested in spirituality today make is to place the impersonal at a higher level than the personal. Abstract being transcends personhood, they think. And yet the truth, proclaimed by revelation and open to the intuition, is the opposite. Personhood is the fullness of being. It is the end to which all abstract being is directed. God is a Person and, even though he might have the aspect of pure being, too, this is a limited part of the totality of what he is. In like manner, it is a limited part of what you are, and if you restrict your spiritual approach to that, you are taking second best. Why not embrace the greater truth?

It should also be noted that many of those who think they can overcome their individuality this way will, in practice, end up deceiving themselves and fall into a fantasy world in which it is the self that has renounced the self. Either they can stay there or else they will have to come back to the idea of God as a person and themselves as his creation.

For these reasons, I see strict non-duality as a flawed philosophy, plausible in terms of Man struggling to grasp the truth about himself and find release from the bondage of identification with the material self and ego, but superseded by the revelation of the Trinity which shows how oneness and multiplicity can coexist without the latter being in any way unreal. Those who think that the spiritual goal is merely to attain to pure consciousness should know that consciousness always has a quality of some sort, just as light always has degrees of brightness, and this should be a matter for rejoicing because it means that our expansion into the life of God can have no conceivable end.

The Atheist Illusion

It is understandable that many people identify as atheists in the contemporary world, given the artificial environment in which we live, the largely out of date form of religion to which we are exposed while growing up (if we are exposed to any at all) and the dominance of a scientific worldview that won't recognise its limitations. However, the truth of the matter is that atheists do not just deny God. In a very real sense they deny themselves. If consciousness arises from material processes then it is mechanical. In a meaningless universe, you have no meaning. Why? Because individuality only has any substance in the context of freedom, and there is no freedom if matter determines mind rather than the other way around.

In fact, the more you assert your right to deny God, the more you maintain his existence.

If you are an atheist it means that you regard life as arising from lifelessness, an odd notion to say the least. It means that fundamentally you must see love as only self-interested, and so without any innate value. It means you deny the sublimity of beauty, for beauty, as opposed to what is just pleasing to the eye, has meaning only to the extent that it points beyond itself to a higher, non-physical reality. That is what moves us to wonder and joy when we perceive it. And it means that, on the moral plane, you see everything as a matter of opinion because there is no objective truth. You may reject these points but they are the natural corollary of your beliefs. You may say that you don't have beliefs but, of course, you do. For a start, you believe that all that can be perceived by the mind and senses is all there is to perceive, a totally irrational supposition. You may say that there is no evidence for a spiritual reality behind the natural world, and point to the many flaws of religion which science has exposed. But science has not exposed any flaws in the substance of religion. It has only shown some of its manmade aspects to be manmade.

As for there being no evidence of a spiritual reality, all one can say is that there are none so blind as those who will not see. Do we discount the evidence of saints and mystics throughout the centuries? Do we reject humanity's highest teachings from its greatest representatives? This may be regarded as circumstantial evidence but, for all the discoveries of science, there is no plausible alternative explanation for life or consciousness or for the strong feeling many of us have deep inside that this world is not our home, and that we are spiritual beings whose source is elsewhere. We can blot this out if we choose but if we do we are denying the substance of our being. And we are betraying our very humanity because the essence of our humanity is that we are more than human. That is to say, more than just the outer aspects of a human being which is all that is acknowledged nowadays.

However, I am not writing this to convince atheists of their error. Rather I would like to support those whose intuitive sensibilities are crushed by the apparent logic of the arguments ranged against spiritual belief. This belief can't be proved by reason alone, and it's not meant to be, but it is not irrational. Spirituality does not deny reason but it does go beyond it for it goes beyond the rational intellect. There was a time when science was the friend of truth. Unfortunately, that is not the case at the moment. Science is now the friend of science. Like the priests of old, scientists guard their power and will not relinquish it without a struggle. I am a lover of science as a servant of God but I reject it when it seeks to supplant God and install itself on his throne with the excuse that if God does not appear to it on its own terms, then he cannot exist.

People say who is this God in whom you believe? Human beings have believed in all sorts of gods, so why is one any more plausible than another? But human beings have tried to express the inexpressible. That is why the forms and perceptions differ. These are necessarily limited by the imagination and understanding of the people who have come up with them. I freely admit that my conception of the spiritual power that transcends the manifested universe, whilst also being present within every atom, is partially determined by my cultural background and personal experiences. But that does not alter the fact that there is a Creator who is the origin of all life in this universe, and who is quite clearly far beyond anything that I or anybody else might conceive. A person might have a spiritual intuition of a greater or lesser degree of intensity, and that gives him an insight into the nature of reality. But that person will have to express the intuition according to the mould of his mind, which may be more or less able to encompass the intuition but will always be limited because the mind is restricted to form which, by definition, has boundaries.

I think there are two sorts of disbelievers in a spiritual reality. There are those, probably the majority, whose inner experience has simply not been sufficient to dislodge the weight of contemporary intellectual opinion. They are victims and not to be condemned except, perhaps, for not thinking a little more deeply about something that is of supreme importance, though some of them may have done just that but simply not been able to come to any conclusion. So they get on with their lives, as one must. It is not necessarily a virtue to believe in God and it can't necessarily be called a vice not to in the present day and age as long as one seeks to live in the highest way one can. It's how you believe or disbelieve that matters, and what you do as a result of that. That having been said, I should add that while a non-believer can still make spiritual progress of a limited kind, this can never go as far or as fast as that of a person who does accept the higher truths and acts accordingly. It's like trying to sail the sea in a leaky boat.

So there are those who don't believe because they see no

reason to believe. But then there are those who actively deny God. Whether through anger or fear or resentment or dislike of the thought that there is a higher power to which they will have to submit, they reject God because they don't like the idea of God. The first category of person simply doesn't know enough but the second category doesn't want to know, and rejects spiritual knowledge on the basis of not wanting it to be true. Naturally, people in this category would never admit this to be the case, preferring to take apparently logical refuge in science, and condemn religion for its outdated and superstitious aspects while completely ignoring its more metaphysical and mystical core. But they are driven by their emotions, and the attachment they have to their prejudices has blinded them to the truth.

We live in a world that appears to have abandoned God but, to all those who yearn for a higher reality than the contemporary world allows, I would say this. Hold fast to your vision. Have faith in an absolute power of goodness and love, and follow the spiritual path in confidence that this world can never extinguish the truth, even if it can sometimes obscure it. All human beings seek God, whether they know it or not, but if you do know it, you are lucky. Pursue that knowledge and do not allow anything to deflect you from the path.

And to the atheist I would say this. Lesser contingent realities can only take their being from a greater self-subsisting reality and truth. If God is not real then nothing is.

Rejecting God

Why do so many human beings want to reject spiritual truth? This is a valid question in the modern age since it is clear that many people who are atheists are so not because of an act of intellect but one of will. The fact of God, a higher power of intelligence and love, who is the source of our being, is graven on every human heart, even if many of us would deny this. It is also apparent from Nature if one looks beneath the surface, and it is taught in religions throughout the world. To be sure, the present materialistic culture and unnatural environment in which we live play a strong part in blinding us to the reality of the Creator, but there is more to it than this. A number of people nowadays are not just casually agnostic or indifferent as to whether there may or may not be a God because they are too busy going about their daily business. They are actively and assertively atheistic. They claim there is no evidence for God (untrue), maintain that science gives them all the answers about life they need (highly disputable since it actually gives none about life and its origin as such) and even condemn religion as morally reprehensible (confusing wrong-headed response to religious teaching with the teaching itself). They say they are motivated entirely by reason, and perhaps some really are mistaken but honest, but there are others who do not want there to be a God or Creator to whom they owe their existence. And these are motivated not so much by reason as intellectual pride and arrogance.

This accusation is not levelled at everyone who doubts a spiritual reality to life. The world is too much with many people, and the idea of God simply doesn't matter to them unless and until they are brought low by suffering. However, there are people who reject God not because of unbelief but because they hate the idea of God and of themselves as created beings. They disguise their true motives, probably even to themselves, which makes it difficult to discuss the matter with them. They are as wedded to their position as a religious fanatic is to his, and anything that conflicts with it is ruled out as inadmissible. Sometimes they will try to be more morally pure than any believer because they need to prove to themselves, and to others, the superiority of their position, and show that they do not need God to be a good or principled person. However, on examination, it transpires that their morality is based precisely on this sense of superiority and arrogance rather than simple goodness, kindness or a genuine concern for others. At best, it is a mentally based morality rather than one of the heart, echoing their own often highly developed intellect but lack of intuitive vision. They are the present day Pharisees.

A confirmed atheist of this kind is an egotist. Of course, a believer may be, too, but, if he is true to his faith, he is at least trying to do something about that. But an active atheist must be so because he has denied God, and the fundamental reason for denying the reality of God is the desire to assert the primacy of the self and be beholden to no one. It is almost a form of teenage rebellion and dislike of being told what to do, which leads me to think that many dogmatic atheists are simply people who have not grown up properly or who carry the wounds of childhood within them, often to the point of not wanting to be healed of these wounds because they feel defined by them; and to be healed would be to lose their sense of self-validating injustice, on the flames of which they feed.

For the truth is atheism is not a reasoned and logical assessment of the situation in which we find ourselves. It is often no more than an angry rejection of God, and denial of the transcendent because of the implications of what that would mean for the atheist's sense of personal autonomy.

Now, of course, some people don't reject God so much as what they believe to be an anthropomorphic version of God, and this is understandable up to a point. Obviously the reality of

God is far beyond any idea we might have about it. But the fact that we are made in his image means that we can, on some level, reflect his reality. This tells us that ideas we might have of him are not completely false as long as they correspond to the highest we can find in ourselves. For instance, when we say that God is a Person we are not saying that he is a person in the same way as Mr Smith who lives next door is a person. He is not a personality but his essential nature is "I", not just pure abstract being. He is 1 (one) but over and above that he is I, the first person.

God, the One Life, cannot be reduced to mere abstract being. For there is no life in the abstract without its instantiation, and those who admit an Absolute without acknowledging a Person are in error. God is life, yes, but more than that he is alive.

The doctrinaire atheist requires everything to be explainable in scientific terms, apparently not noticing that a great deal of our experience lies outside the limitations imposed by the senses, which is the world explored, often in extraordinary detail, by science. But what this leads to is a denial of such things as goodness, beauty and truth as being in any way real. They become merely relative things, simple concepts or personal judgments, which evaporate when you look at them too closely. Now, there are no solid, intellectual grounds for doing this so it can only be a prejudice. The prejudice springs from a desire, and the desire is to reject God because the person does not want to think of himself as a creature, a created being accountable for his actions to a judge who has authority over him. He wants to be free but the freedom he wants is of and for the self. However, to be bound by and to the self is the greatest captivity. The only true freedom is from the self, and this is only possible in God.

Then there is the question of morality. The atheist justifies his rejection of God by saying that he needs no spiritual overlord to make him behave properly. He has a moral system based on reason which is just as humane and decent as any spiritual morality. Leaving aside the fact that his secular morality is often based on his inheritance of a spiritual one, and that, in many respects, it becomes progressively weaker the further it departs from its original source, there are other problems that he may not have considered as thoroughly as he should.

Most people in the modern world grow up in households in which the prevailing moral ideas are shaped by a type of secular humanism, which might appear not too different to Christianity if that were a religion purely of this world with no sense of the next. This is not surprising since, as I say, secular humanism has borrowed much of its moral position from Christianity, but it leads many people to think that secular humanism has taken all the important bits of Christianity and got rid of the superfluous stuff. The truth is the other way round.

What is left out is the reality of a transcendent absolute, and this is the foundation of all the rest. Without the fatherhood of God, the brotherhood of man has nothing real to bind it together and the undoubted moral falling away in the West and elsewhere comes from replacing a morality rooted in spiritual truth with a secular morality that has no roots in anything real. The result is that each generation becomes further separated from the idea of spiritual truth and, as it does, its sense of a genuine moral order, founded on a real, transcendent truth is diminished.

Once you start to separate human intellect and will and feelings from their proper source in spiritual realities, you lose the all-important connection between the human being as he is here in this world and his true origin and purpose which are in higher dimensions of existence.

For the fact is that the basis for an objective standard of morality can only come from something eternal that is outside the human mind. This is God and it must be a personal God, too, because impersonal reality would be truth only whereas a full and complete morality needs to be based on love and truth equally, and that means a personal God. Only if founded on a transcendent reality can morality itself be real in the sense of being the same at all times and in all places, and not contingent on external factors. But any morality that comes from the human mind will inevitably be conditional and dependent on circumstances affecting that mind. In consequence it will be both mutable and relative.

Secular morality denies religion so it has to look elsewhere to justify itself. Often, nowadays, it looks to science but science can only examine the realm of nature, and nature cannot explain itself, so science has nothing to say about true morality. This is an inversion of truth in which the tail is seen to be wagging the dog. No wonder it gets everything back to front. And when it comes down to it, the very phrase "secular morality" is a contradiction in terms since secular means something of this world while morality, if it is to be grounded in anything real, necessarily implies something beyond this world, something that takes its origin from a timeless reality of truth and goodness. If there is not this reality then any system of behaviour is arbitrary and meaningless, and one is not better than another from an absolute point of view. This leaves you with a morality that can change at any time, and a changing morality is no morality at all.

The point I am making here does not mean that an atheist can never act from a moral position. Of course he can, but what I am saying is that if he does, and that position coincides with what is generally accepted as goodness, he can have no real reason for doing so according to his belief of how reality is structured. Indeed, without some kind of sense of an absolute that overrides everything in this world, and against which everything in this world must be measured, how can the atheist actually define anything as "good" as such? His belief, logically considered, must mean that there is no real moral difference between a Hitler and a saint. Each is just pursuing his own subjective preference and there is no proper reason to say that one is better or worse than the other. Against what true yardstick would you be measuring this? The common good? But there is no common good if all we are is animated matter. Without an over-arching reality we are all just locked in our little selves with no true connection to anybody else. Consequently there is no real reason for me to care about you except for any advantage it might bring me. And what this adds up to is that a secular morality has no foundation outside or beyond itself, and therefore can never be truly real.

Morality, Secular and Spiritual

It is sometimes claimed that as intelligence has increased, so we have also become more moral. Setting aside whether intelligence has really increased or whether our brains and thought patterns have simply been educated into the modern technological way of thinking, good in some respects, poor in others, this assertion must surely depend on what kind of morality one espouses. For me, or anyone acknowledging a spiritual reality, morality is first and foremost about loving truth and attempting to coordinate oneself to that. And this means knowing, to some degree at least, what truth is. Hence the secular humanist morality, being largely atheistic as it denies or ignores the spiritual reality, is almost the least moral attitude one can take. This implies that much of the perceived improvement is merely a matter of greater conformity to the prejudices and ideologies of the day.

Every society or culture must have some kind of morality or else it will collapse. Its morality will be based on its formational mythology, and in the case of contemporary Western culture that mythology is rooted in the ideals of the 18th century Enlightenment on the one hand, and the theory of evolution on the other. Both of these, if they don't actually dismiss a Creator, certainly pave the way for his dismissal. So you could say that our modern morality is based largely on the assumption that there is only humanity, and human obligations and duties and responsibilities are only to other humans. This is not wholly true because many of the moral ideas that fed into and shaped this belief system were actually inherited from Christianity, even if this is often unacknowledged today, but it is the way modern secular morality tends to perceive itself.

Now, this basing of morality, and how we approach life, ourselves and others, on a purely humanistic level may seem to have much to recommend it, but if it arises from an incorrect or even downright wrong view of the world then it is insufficient, to say the least. It may even be, in some respects, immoral.

For a proper morality has two strands, a vertical and a horizontal, and these are plainly identified by Jesus in his two commandments. To love God with all your heart and all your soul and all your mind, and to love your neighbour as yourself. These sum up the essence of any morality based on truth, but here's the interesting thing. It is no accident that the commandments were given in that order because if the second is to be in any sense real, then it must grow out of the first. That is to say, the love of man, if genuine, can only really derive from the love of God, and this is because what you are loving is not man in himself but God in man. For God is both the source of love and its end. There is no other. If he is not present then whatever feeling you might think you have, it is not love, not in its true, spiritual sense. And love is spiritual in origin. Anything that is not spiritually derived is not love. We may think it is but that only means we do not know love but merely its reflection as it appears in our mind in this world.

So we can only really love our neighbour if first we love God. Without this divine love we can have good will or fellow feeling towards our neighbour but not love, and, in the long run, only love can overcome the ego and so bring about a morality that is true and innate rather than a mainly intellectual or ideologically derived thing that can, and will, crack under pressure.

What this means is that our modern morality, which only acknowledges the horizontal, cannot be properly effective even on that level. The first moral requirement is to love God. Everything else springs from that, from the vertical, and if that love is not present, or at least an awareness of the need for it, then any morality is flawed and will eventually fail. I am not disputing that the modern approach to morality has improved on the past in some respects. Exclusive focus on the horizontal will necessarily bring certain areas into greater prominence, and they may benefit thereby. However, these material improvements (which is what they are) take on much less significance once you realise that this approach has lost sight of the essential, for it is founded on a falsehood, namely the primacy of Man. But if morality should really be seen in the light of God, the soul and eternity rather than that of man and woman as they appear to be in this mortal world, well, that puts everything in a rather different perspective, doesn't it?

I have said that a true morality must have a vertical and a horizontal component, and that the latter must derive from the former. The atheist might dispute this (atheists love to argue!) and say he can have a perfectly good morality without bringing God into the equation. Perhaps he can but, without an absolute reference point, what does he base his morality on? For when God is banished from reality there can be no morality resting on something real, but only one that depends on opinion and preference. If there is not something that stands above us and unites us by virtue of its transcendence and its absoluteness, then there is no unchanging right or wrong. There is only custom, convention and what is deemed to suit a particular society at any given moment. If we are just the product of a directionless, purposeless, meaningless evolution, as the atheist and materialist have to believe, then nothing really matters, nothing is true and nothing is better than anything else. A human being is not the crown of creation and the means through which incarnate earthly life may transform and transcend itself, but just one material form among many. As for the individual human being, each one is isolated and locked in itself with no real connection to any other human being. Morality is just a theoretical thing, utilitarianism by any other name, with no relationship to any kind of universal truth because there is none.

This is why it might reasonably be said that the only truly moral position is to acknowledge God, or certainly to acknowledge a real and eternal transcendent principle. Without this foundation no worldly morality can stand for long. It's built on sand. Conversely, to deny God might be considered an immoral act: indeed it might just be the most immoral act. First of all, because it denies truth and substitutes that with a lie, but secondly, because it does away with the only real support for a moral system that has any meaning beyond the purely practical. I am not claiming here that a believer is automatically a better person than a non-believer, but a genuine believer has at least opened himself up to some form of truth while, in contrast, a non-believer has closed himself off from truth.

Without God morality is just opinion.

God and Science

In modern times science has become the chief idol of humanity. It is seen as the only reliable means to knowledge, both of the world and of ourselves. It alone gives truth, or so runs the contemporary narrative. But what if it were a false idol (all idols are false, of course) and led not to an increased understanding of life but to a narrowing of vision, a loss of true values and eventual death? That is my view but it is definitely a heretical one according to the accepted canons of modern belief. It would not only be dismissed as absurd and ignorant by secular authorities, but would also be rejected by many religious leaders who fail to see that if you try to ride two horses going in different directions, one of them will inevitably have to follow the other.

So why is science so highly regarded and why do I reject its authority? To answer the second question first, it's very simple. I reject its authority because it is wrong. If science were not materialistic by default, that would not be the case but it is or certainly has become so. Therefore it denies all truths not open to its own limited means of research. It has identified itself so completely with materialism that it cannot break that connection without diminishing itself and its unique authority. Individual scientists do not necessarily all think in this way but the discipline as a whole does.

So, to be clear, I do not reject science so much as its materialistic bias, but nowadays the two are locked so closely together that they cannot be prised apart. And I reject this bias on practically every ground I can think of, be it those one would expect such as tradition, revelation, religion, experience, intuition, imagination, faith, but also those that are regarded with approval by scientists themselves such as reason and logic. For materialism is irrational in that it can explain nothing fundamental in itself but still won't accept the obvious, namely that the universe is set up and governed by intelligence. It has to deny this intelligence because to accept it would be to undermine its own position of pre-eminence. Thus when science looks behind the veil of existence at such root realities as life, consciousness and intelligence, never mind all those troublesome things not definable in terms of mathematics like beauty, love and goodness, all it sees is basically nothing. Literally nothing real in the latter case (i.e. these things are just subjective) and nothing existing independently of determining material processes in the former.

As for why science is highly regarded, there are various reasons. Firstly, it is relatively new. According to our current way of looking at the world anything recent is likely to be seen as more advanced than what came before. As, in some respects, it may be. Then there is no doubt that science, through its practical application of technology, has changed the world radically and, in many ways, for the better. It has got results and made our lives much easier. It has also explained some things that were mysteries and corrected some ideas that were incorrectly understood. It has vastly increased our intellectual understanding of the physical and, to some extent, psychological worlds. All this is undeniable. But there is also the equally undeniable fact that science appeals to those who wish to reject God, which means those who are motivated by pride in their own independent intellects. From this perspective, at least, science can be viewed as a product of the Fall, and one, I don't say directly inspired by, but certainly exploited by that being who was the agent of the Fall and the first to reject the authority of the Creator.

Even those who recognise that science has overstepped its boundaries from the 19th century onwards like to say that this is not the fault of science as such. It is simply a misuse of science. But I wonder if the aspect of misuse is not actually implicit in the discipline itself. Science, after all, is something that depends on the analysis of the material world and the use of the rational mind. It is fundamentally anti-spiritual in its conception from the outset so unless it submits itself to a higher authority, whether that be God, the soul, revelation or spiritual intuition, it will always end up in the way it has. And the majority of its adherents will always resist anything that threatens their hegemony and position on top of the intellectual pile.

What science basically does is break things up in order to look inside them. That is the way it understands them. Now this can be very effective up to a point but something essential is lost along the way. What that is may be hard to define, especially in scientific terms because it is not open to the scientific method of exploration. But we can call it the soul or quality of the thing, and anybody with the slightest bit of imagination will know what that means. But science won't accept imagination as in any way pointing to reality because it operates outside of its domain.

I am not dismissing the scientific approach but I am saying that, taken to excess, as it is now, it is highly damaging to the proper development of a human being. It must be accompanied by, in fact subordinated to, a more visionary mode of perception which approaches things intuitively, and is able to look behind and beyond externals without chopping them up into their component parts but seeing them as whole. Science may be able to manipulate matter but it cannot see the reality of which matter is only an expression.

If we take the birth of science in the modern sense as being in the 17th century (a somewhat arbitrary date but more or less accurate) we can see that, whatever the reasons for its initial awakening in the Western consciousness, it soon began to regard itself as the rival to religion rather than its companion and ally. The spiritual worldview, founded on faith, which, properly understood, is the openness that encourages the development of intuition, was replaced by a strictly rational approach that rejected anything that could not be confirmed by the senses or proved by reason. I simplify to make a point but this is a broadly correct description of what took place during the course of the 18th and 19th centuries.

Scientists came to believe that mathematics could describe reality, failing to see that mathematics can only describe that limited aspect of reality which it describes, which aspect is but a fraction of the whole: one that leaves out great swathes of reality, including the essential part. This non-measurable part is known through the imagination and intuition, confirmed by scripture and revelation, and can be accessed by following the traditional spiritual path and disciplines. However, as it is beyond form and quantity, it falls outside investigation by a science which limits itself to the external world or that which is immediately apparent to the senses and mind. Science simply denied what it could not investigate by its own methods, and rejected any other methods or means of approach to reality. It hobbled itself because of its lack of vision, and also, perhaps, because of a desire for power. It even started to become the authoritarian church that it had originally tried to contest. The religious worldview of the time needed to be supplemented or balanced, but balance requires equilibrium and pretty soon the scales became weighted far too heavily on the side that favoured fact over meaning.

Now we have a situation in which the scientific worldview is the orthodox one, and heretics are either ridiculed (which admittedly is better than being burned) or dismissed as unintelligent. Even religious people, other than fundamentalists, give precedence to science in more and more areas because they have grown up in a world in which we are all conditioned by the authorities to follow a certain way of thinking. Sometimes they even do this to the extent of allowing it to determine how much or how little space should be accorded to their religious beliefs. The undoubted achievements of science on the technological side, and the fact that it has made our material lives considerably more comfortable also influence us to give it our intellectual allegiance when perhaps we should be more discerning.

For there is a problem. Notwithstanding its achievements in the material world and its exposure of much superstition and ignorance, modern science rests on a falsehood because it denies, or sees no reason to acknowledge, metaphysical reality. That is not the way it would look at itself but it is a truth known to anyone who, either intuitively or through faith, sees that the basis of life is spiritual. This has enormous consequences for how we understand and live in the world, but it also means that science doesn't even understand its own field of operation, the material plane. Why? Because without metaphysical knowledge you cannot even comprehend the natural world properly as you will see what you expect to see according to your pre-existing assumptions which, in the case of modern science, are entirely materialistic.

This is why I maintain that the adoption of the scientific worldview is such a disaster for humanity. I say this because it has resulted in a catastrophic separation of Man from his true being. It has cut us adrift from spiritual reality and led us into an unrecognised hubris, the hubris of a creature that denies its Creator. Now, it is true that the great majority of people are passive victims of this mind-set, it being the accepted orthodoxy of the day and therefore hard to resist. But there are some who are active promulgators of this false doctrine and they, whether they know it or not, are doing the devil's work. Quite possibly because they share his main vice and besetting sin which is intellectual pride.

For, as we have seen, some atheists are so not for supposed rational reasons but because they do not want to live in a universe in which there is a God. One in which they will have to acknowledge a Creator. And these people use science to bolster their prejudice, not for a disinterested view of the matter. And they can do this because science is not disinterested, not disinterested enough anyway, as it wants to extend the field in which it has power and authority as far as possible, squeezing out any rival it may have in terms of knowledge. Since religion and metaphysics claim an authority beyond the realm open to science, they must be dismissed as archaic relics from humanity's childhood.

There are, of course, plenty of scientists dedicated to the pursuit of truth as they see it but they are fatally handicapped by the basic materialistic premise of science as it is understood today, as well as their over-reliance on the human intellect. This is why I maintain that the dogmas of science corrupt the mind. For science is concerned only with outer things, but outer things are transient and ultimately unreal, except considered as the expression of inner spiritual archetypes which are the only true reality. Consequently scientists will never get to grips with the true nature of things until they abandon their prejudices and preconceptions, and humble themselves before the divine.

None of the points I raise here mean that I don't recognise that, in the greater scheme of things, and in the context of the times in which it arose, science had its part to play. However, we are currently trapped in a period of over-dominance by science, and its basic premise is a profound metaphysical error that needs correcting. The good that a purely earthbound science could do, it has done. The evil that it has brought about now needs to be addressed. Humanity needs to move on into a future in which science will still play its part, but only once it has been radically reformed and brought into line with spiritual wisdom. There is no doubt that it has helped correct previous errors but it is now responsible for the greatest error of all, which is the denial of spiritual truth. Science, if it is to serve humanity, must be purged of its materialism.

We live in times of great spiritual ignorance and anyone who sees that has a responsibility to point it out. However, I am not writing to attack anyone but to support those whose intuitions are petrified at source by the culture in which they live. Increasingly, materialistic science assumes the status of orthodox dogma and dissenting voices are marginalised. I think of children growing up with little or no exposure to religious teaching and nothing to nourish their spiritual imaginations. Is it over-dramatic to consider this a crime? Some atheists claim it's a crime to teach young children about a spiritual world when there's no proof (to their way of thinking) that such a thing exists, but what if it does and access to it is withheld? What then? What if children are not even given the opportunity, through lack of information, to believe in a spiritual reality? Is this not a form of abuse?

In fact, I regard the very question "Do you believe in God?" to be a wrong one, since it implies an unbiased choice can be made in this matter. Often the way a question is framed contains certain inbuilt assumptions and preconceptions which have an influence on the answer. As far as God is concerned, it is not a question of belief. God is a fact, so the question should not be "Do you believe in God" but "Do you see the reality of God?" The truth of God is stamped in every heart and either we acknowledge that or we don't. Doubt is permissible, but to actively deny God is generally a sign of pride.

Despite my polemic here about modern science, I would not want it to be thought that I have no appreciation for the revolution in thinking it brought about. When the scientific method first arose, it brought a fresh approach to the study of reality, which study is one reason for our existence on this Earth. Old ways had become stale, corrupted by superstitions and false beliefs, even if the truth was still there under several centuries' worth of man-made accretions. Ignorance abounded in many departments of life, but it's hardly worth me saying that as it's obvious. We needed science to clear away intellectual cobwebs and stimulate new ways of thinking, never mind the technological advancements which have liberated humanity in many ways even if they have enslaved us in others, which is becoming ever more apparent. I would never dispute any of that. But the fact remains that science exceeded its brief. It may have corrected wrongs and imbalances of the past, but it created new ones. It may have given us great power over nature, but it robbed us of a spiritual home. It expanded certain horizons but it lost the centre. It opened the mind to new ways of thinking, but ruthlessly closed off the old ones when we needed a balance between the two. The problem, then, is not science, but scientists not acknowledging the limitations of their science, and stepping beyond their legitimate boundaries.

Science, considered as the system of knowledge we have today, can be regarded as a step on the journey that leads humanity from the consciousness in which subject and object are not yet experienced separately, the so-called participation consciousness, to one in which they are completely separate (now) to one in which there is the fully conscious, direct perception of spiritual union. It was a necessary step in the separation of consciousness from its primeval state of being embedded in nature, begun long ago but only completed relatively recently. However, it forgot the basic rule of the new which is that it should incorporate the best of the old. The old ways should not have been rejected but assimilated, and then integrated with the new. You might think it inevitable that, for the new to be established properly, the old should be discarded but it need not have been so. If science had not reduced the imagination to a purely subjective faculty, if it had respected the integrity of the whole human being, if it had not looked at nature from a quantitative point of view, and if it had not pursued power and control to the degree that it did, then it might not have made the errors it has made.

So science was a liberating force in many respects, certainly to begin with, but the 18th century Enlightenment was not all one way. It also brought in its train a darkening of consciousness in some areas with the result that materialistic scientists are now the ones preventing proper progress. They are the modern-day believers in a flat earth, for the world they have created is a barren wasteland, stripped of meaning and without true hope. We may not see it that way because we are seduced by the technological appliances that science has provided us with, and lulled into a false sense of ease by the physical comfort its discoveries in the material world have given us. But these will ultimately prove to be without real substance. Scientists have forgotten that knowledge must always be subordinate to truth. They need to open their minds to the greater reality that lies beyond their instruments, equations and theories, and perceive the world as the expression of a Divine Intelligence. Only then can their science become a pure approach to the world and be what it should be, which is a hymn of praise to the Creator.

Science means knowledge. That's all it means. It is, therefore, good. The pursuit of knowledge is a large part of what it is to be human. It is our destiny and duty to seek to know. But, as every spiritual aspirant understands, there is a knowledge of the head and one of the heart, and contemporary science focuses entirely on the former while ignoring the latter. The knowledge of the head is made of individual pieces connected together, and built up gradually by rational means, but the knowledge of the heart is direct perception. And, while the first means that the knower and his knowledge are always separate, in the knowledge of the heart they are one. The knower is his knowledge and vice versa. Our contemporary science needs to rediscover this truth and realise that true knowledge, which is the knowledge of inner realities, can only come from the heart. That is not to dismiss outer knowledge but simply to point out that it is outer, and that the head can have knowledge but it can never know truth.

Thus we can say that science is a noble pursuit when practiced with the idea that behind physics there is metaphysics, but when practiced without that vision, or the clear understanding that the natural world is but the outward manifestation of a greater spiritual reality, it will not lead to the more abundant life but only to death.

Let me leave the last word to the Masters. "**Reason less and accept more. It is not necessary to chase after the many mysteries of existence. Live simply in the heart and all mysteries will in time become known to you. Do not be as those who seek to penetrate to every corner of the universe but do not know themselves**." This is advice scientists would do well to consider.

Creation and Evolution

Science can never truly understand the world because when it looks at it what it sees is a reflection of its own way of looking. The information it gleans from the world cannot go beyond the limitations of its reason based approach because all that approach can uncover is the part of life that is open to it. Higher levels of existence that are not accessible to reason and sensory observation simply can't be detected. So it is not that science sees what it wants to see, but what it sees is all it can see because what is observed is determined by what is observing and how it observes. A fly sees the world according to the limitations of its mind, and so does a scientist. The difference is that the fly can't help it but the modern scientist imposes these restrictions on himself because he denies a faculty higher than reason. Now, reason is certainly not a false faculty. It is God-given, but when it is taken as man's highest faculty and its existence is used to reject higher spiritual principles, then the servant has become master, and so reason becomes a tyrant that insists the world is seen according to its own limitations.

If we note how modern science started, we can see the near inevitability of its descent into spiritual ignorance. For nature to be regarded solely as an object of study and exploitation it was separated from its roots in the spiritual world, a world not open to investigation by the new methods. As time passed and the new approach proved highly successful in material terms, it came to be seen as the only way in which the world could be understood, despite the protestations of people like William Blake and writers and artists associated with the Romantic movement of the late 18th and early 19th centuries. When science, through Darwinism, came up with its own theory of human origins its triumph was assured, and we now live with the spiritually disastrous results of that. Even much spirituality nowadays, such as it is, has to accord with science if it is to be accepted as realistic.

Anyone taking the line I have here will inevitably be asked if (for example) he uses computers or avails himself of the advantages of modern medicine. In other words, if he uses some of the many benefits that science has brought. If the answer is yes, he will be charged with hypocrisy. However, it's not that simple. We all live in the 21st century and, unless we take to the woods and become hermits, we have to do so. No one disputes that modern science has brought many material benefits. It would never have made the impact it has if it had not done so, but the point is, it has brought them at a spiritual cost. If we live in the modern world then we more or less have to use the products of science, and we can legitimately do so, though I would suggest we should do so to a limited degree if we wish to avoid being contaminated by the mind-set behind them, that being the idea that basically man is little different to a machine. This is the great and largely unrecognised risk that our ever increasing dependence on technology brings with it. It is not too much to say that this dependence is actually restructuring our minds and rendering them less and less susceptible to spiritual influence. The more we use machines, the more we become like them.

Thus I say that, while science has brought some good things on the material level (it has brought many bad and unholy things, too) these don't compensate for the spiritual destruction it has wrought. And yet it is not science as such that I am attacking, but a science not pursued in the light of the reality of God and the hierarchical supremacy of revelation and spiritual insight to unsupported reason. If science acknowledged that there are truths, deeper, foundational truths, beyond its reach then it might begin to acquire a wisdom it currently lacks, and which we so desperately need. If it pursued knowledge not for its own sake or even humanity's sake, but for a fuller revelation of God, then it might start to discover something really worthwhile.

The question of Man's origins is one on which science has pronounced. Although a belief in God is just about compatible with full acceptance of the theory of evolution, a good deal has to be given up and the religious person immediately puts himself on the back foot. Once there he is on a downward path, forced to concede more and more because he has accepted the framework of his opponent. But there is really no need to do this, for the theory of evolution only addresses outer, material things, and, besides, it makes many unprovable assumptions. In truth, it can only be believed by someone who wants to believe it, or else someone who, deferring to the professionals, simply assumes that science knows what it is talking about. No one, except out and out fundamentalists, would deny that evolution as described is an element of how life has changed, but from that to conclude it is the only element is an unjustified leap.

I regard this question of our origins as something of a litmus test for spiritually interested people in that it examines their response to the wisdom of this world, plus their ability to remain connected to higher truths when these are not conventionally accepted: indeed, when they are actively rejected by most people. Often each side in the creation/evolution debate totally dismisses the position of the other but, for my part, I don't regard evolution and creation to be inherently incompatible, though obviously, in that case, neither can be taken in the exclusive way their materialist and fundamentalist proponents would take them.

The way I approach this matter is through a combination of intuition and ordinary thinking, the one supporting the other. However, for me, intuition always takes precedence as that is based on direct perception, based on inner connection to the truth of things, and goes beyond a strictly reason based approach which can only examine reality from the outside looking in.

I think we must start from the position that there has obviously been some sort of evolutionary process at work over the ages. The findings of science leave little room for doubt on that score. From there, though, to conclude that this is just driven by random genetic mutation and survival of the fittest is going way too far, and rather suggests that the wish is father to the thought. Which is not to say that these play no part in the process, particularly in the non-human kingdoms, only that they are not the primary mechanism. Even if we set intuition aside, common sense should tell us that natural selection, alone and unaided, simply cannot account for the world and everything in it, however long one allows it, and that means that evolution is not blind. It has a purpose and it has a goal. As for mankind, we are not just intelligent apes but a creation that was deliberately brought about to reconcile and integrate the two opposites in the universe of spirit and matter or consciousness and the phenomenal world, the world within and the world out there: breath and dust, as one might say. An animal lives exclusively in its natural environment. It cannot separate itself from that, but our glory (and the source of our short-term misery and suffering) is that we live in two worlds. Even though we are part of nature we have an inner life, and through that can eventually unite spirit and matter in full consciousness and, in the process of doing so, become fully conscious participants in a creation which is differentiated but one. All this is not the product of a directionless evolution, but an evolutionary process helps to bring it about.

What this means is that I see evolution as a blend of intelligence, purpose and will on the one hand – there is a plan and there is a goal – and what we may call chance on the other as the laws of nature work out in the ways currently envisaged by biologists. That is to say, overall there is direction by a Divine Intelligence but within that there is a good deal of flexibility and room for variation in line with the accepted principles of contemporary evolutionary understanding. Consequently I see the human form as brought to its current state (doubtless from pre-existing material) as a specific vehicle for spiritual beings to gain the experience needed for the growth of their consciousness. It has not come about purely by chance. I see no contradiction between the idea that the forms we use have their prototype on an archetypal level, and that they come into being on this physical level through a mixture of natural process and spiritual direction. So we might think of our original form as initially precipitated onto this plane from a spiritual one, but then adapted once it is here.

I also see men and women as descended spiritual beings in human form rather than having ascended up through the animal kingdom – even though the outer bodies they use may have started off doing just that. And I draw a clear distinction between animals and human beings, seeing the latter as possessing the spiritual self-reflective principle while the former does not, though it may well be evolving towards a state in which it does: in which, metaphysically speaking, it earns a soul.

So evolution as we understand it today is a half-truth. As an explanation of how life forms change and develop it has much to recommend it. As an explanation of life itself, of consciousness and of the origin of human beings, it is completely mistaken.

Therefore we can say that evolution is a good explanation for the profusion and variety of many of the animal forms to be found in nature, but does not account for the basic template which exists as something like a Platonic archetype and then manifests in the physical world according to various means, some of which are those described by modern science. This is actually hinted at in the Biblical account of creation in Genesis when it says "Let the earth bring forth living creatures" i.e. it is the earth or natural forces that do this not the Creator directly. Hence I regard evolution principally as an unfolding (which, after all, is what the word actually means) of an intrinsic and always present pattern, just as the tree unfolds from the seed and in some way is already present in the seed. This does not rule out the variations on a theme which would come about in the way we know, but these are the workings out in matter from a pre-existing divine template. They concern substance not essence, which is to say, outer forms but not Form itself, the inner divine pattern.

To sum up in a sentence, natural selection clearly has a part in the evolutionary process but it is very much secondary to the unfolding from within of the pre-existing spiritual pattern.

Despite its insights, modern evolutionary theory is a classic circular argument in that it assumes a conclusion, materialism, in order to reach that conclusion. In fact, it has become little more than a creation myth for atheists, materialists and those who don't want to think too seriously about their origin. As seems to be increasingly the case nowadays in many branches of life, it takes an aspect of the truth and makes of it the whole truth. It elevates a part, relatively minor at that, to the whole, and this it clearly does because of an unadmitted desire to cut free from the perceived limitations of religion. But this desire has blinded many evolutionists to the partiality of their position and the fact that, when all is said and done, it rests entirely on the massive supposition that, given enough time, anything can happen.

The fact is that God works in the world through a mixture of freedom and necessity, just as he does on the individual level through free will and destiny. This means that he sets up basic laws and parameters, and lets them take their course. These laws determine the fundamental building blocks of existence but they allow for an element of chance, which makes the whole process more interesting.

So far in this chapter I don't think I have said anything which is too much of a stretch for the imagination. But I'd like to conclude with a brief speculation. Could evolution be driven from two directions? That is, outwardly, in the way proposed by science, and inwardly by angels? Of these the second is much the more important. The angels would be the builders of form and designers of the body. Their task would be to provide suitable vehicles for the development of consciousness with the secondary aim of creating beauty, though with God there is no conflict between the useful and the beautiful. Consequently it is the angels who brought about the upright stance, the larger brain, the dexterity of hands, the ability to form the sounds of speech and so forth. These things did not arise by chance but were the body's response to inner angelic inspiration. They are what makes a man start to become a god.

God and Suffering

Why is the world such a terrible place? Anyone inclined to a belief in God must have asked this question at one time or another. It points to a problem that prevents many people from accepting there is a spiritual reality behind outer appearance. This can lead to discouragement and the attitude that there is really little need to try to make oneself a better person. Just eat, drink and be merry and so on. But if we could understand why the world is not as ideal as we might like it to be, that would remove one of the main obstacles to belief. It would give meaning and purpose to our existence, and what is life without meaning and a higher purpose than the satisfaction of personal aims which, even if achieved, never bring lasting content?

I was once asked this question in the following form.

Q. Why is the world such a terrible place? Why did God, if he exists, not create it perfect? Doesn't the fact that it's so imperfect support the materialistic thesis that it arose in a random way rather than an ordered one? I once heard a naturalist talk about a worm that burrows into the eye of a child somewhere in Africa, and how he couldn't believe in a God in a world in which such things happened.

This is a reasonable question given our experience in the world but it can be answered. Here is the reply I gave at the time.

"Have you ever considered the possibility that maybe the world was created perfect, as in the story of the Garden of Eden, and that it is fallen human consciousness that has afflicted it? Traditional spiritual teachings say that when man fell, he dragged nature down with him because his consciousness affects or, in this case, corrupts his environment. Incidentally, this is why our current materialistic attitudes actually make our world more material, and why altering our attitude to life is so important. But, setting this aside, the point is that Earth nowadays is a school so it is not intended to be perfect, if by that you mean all good. There is choice, and there is good and evil as a result of that. You might even consider that perhaps the Earth is perfect as an environment for the growing of consciousness as we are given the opportunity for a variety of experiences here. That's not to say we can't make it better or worse, but to expect this world to be a paradise is to misunderstand its purpose.

Besides, is the world so terrible? There are bad things in it but that may be because the purpose of it is to provide choice so that we may grow. Therefore the possibility of distorting the light must exist. But the light, which is the basis to everything, is good. Bad things only exist as corruptions of good things. They have no intrinsic reality in themselves."

Let me now develop that brief overview of the problem of God and suffering, and see if the undeniable presence of the latter can be squared with the existence of the former. In fact, the two are not at all contradictory as I hope to show.

I will begin by mentioning a television interview in 2015 with the actor Stephen Fry in which he referred to any God who might have created this world as "an evil and capricious monster". This predictably stirred up all sorts of excitement with believers quick to damn him and fellow atheists eagerly cheering him on. But, setting aside the extravagant nature of his language, any fair-minded observer would have to concede that he had a point. How could a God that is good have created a world in which there is so much suffering? Not just the suffering inflicted by human beings on each other, which could reasonably be put down to the result of the gift of free will, but the suffering actually inherent in nature. The sicknesses of children is the usual example given in these cases, and it's the one that was used here. Of course, to use this particular example does rather smack of emotional manipulation, but the point is made.

We should observe first of all that there is nothing new in the accusation. Why there is evil, why there is suffering, why there is so much imperfection in nature are all questions that have long been asked, and they are ones that anyone who posits a supernatural origin to this world must address. They can't just be dismissed as unknowables whose purpose will become clearer later on. They must be acknowledged, and an attempt made to explain them now, even if the truth of the matter is that their full significance will probably only become apparent after we have left this world. It is just a fact that we are not given all the answers in this life. Our capacity to respond to the truth that is inscribed in our hearts is tested, as that is the way we develop spiritually and become more identified with the spiritual soul and less with the self-centred mind. Sometimes we do have to proceed on faith, much as the modern temperament may revolt against that, and we have to do so because attunement to the spiritual world requires an open channel. That doesn't mean that we should suspend reason or intellect, but nor must we close the mind to what is beyond it.

That is why I think we are better off taking the reality of God as a given, and then trying to work out the meaning of suffering in this context rather than just using the fact of suffering as an excuse to dismiss God. This attitude may seem like a cheat, but then suffering is not the only ingredient in the mix of this world. There is love, there is beauty, there is the mystery of life and consciousness themselves, and there is the testimony of practically all human beings from all cultures throughout history which cannot just be dismissed as superstitious ignorance. As a matter of fact, I believe that everyone knows in their hearts that there is a God, but many of us, for a variety of reasons, deny this in our heads, which is where most of us live most of the time. And that is why someone like Stephen Fry can seem to be so angry with God. Why be angry with a non-existent being? Does he suspect God might exist, but doesn't like the implications of this?

However that is just speculation on my part. I have no insight into the reasons for his rejection of God. What I would say is that a common reason for this rejection is the dislike people have of being told what to do coupled with the feeling that they might be being judged if they go against the rules. Needless to say, that is fundamentally to misunderstand the nature of the divine. There is truth and there is anti-truth but to obey truth means to fulfil our true nature and leads to the greatest happiness. It is to conform to what is real. To go against truth is to go against reality, and leads not to judgment, as in condemnation and punishment by a dictatorial overlord, but to the same inevitable consequences that follow the letting go of a stone in mid-air. The stone will fall. Why rail against the laws of God if you don't rail against the laws of gravity? What needs to be understood is that these laws are not coercive but lie at the very roots of our being and define what we truly and genuinely are. It is only the ego that rebels against them. In actual fact, to obey them is the only real freedom. For freedom is the ability to do consciously what is right.

I may seem to have gone off the point a bit here but the active rejection of God is often founded on a psychological maladjustment, and it's necessary to expose this if we are fully to answer the question of why there is suffering, and see why that question is posed in the first place. You might think that it is posed because there *is* suffering but, to return to the point made earlier, that is not a sufficient reason to reject the idea of a Creator outright, given the many other extraordinary and unexplained characteristics of existence. There is suffering in life but that is by no means all life is or even anywhere near most of what life is. It is an aspect of life and must be seen in an overall context, one in which the positives considerably outweigh the negatives, as I'm sure even dyed-in-the-wool atheists would agree. Still, the question must be asked. Why is there suffering in life at all if this world is the creation of a perfect and loving God?

There are, in fact, several answers to that question, all of which tie in together to give a full and complete explanation for the imperfect state of our world. To begin with, it is worth considering whether, as some teachings affirm, the platform of this world was not created by God directly, but by high spiritual beings or angelic powers who were carrying out God's will but on their own level of understanding and ability, which may have been far beyond anything we might conceive but was still not perfect. This is point one and may be regarded as academic, given it certainly does not explain, still less justify, suffering, but it is worth making.

Point two is more relevant. It introduces the human element. The world now is not as it was originally intended to be and at one time was. It may have been created perfect, or as perfect as it could be within the limitations mentioned above as well as those imposed by matter itself, which inevitably tends to disorder and disintegration because only spirit is really real and anything less will eventually revert to that. But it is now a fallen world, and it is so because of human beings whose disequilibrium has spread throughout the whole of nature. Now, whether this is just the result of a necessary temporary focus on self and the separation from oneness which results from that, as some believe, or whether it is because of something actually having gone wrong in the distant past, as the book of Genesis implies and the existence of free will makes possible, is perhaps of secondary importance. This world has fallen away from what it should have been and into corruption because of the activity of human beings. Because they rebelled against the divine order. Of course, we are still doing that.

Taken together these two ideas could reconcile the apparent opposites of a benevolent Creator and the imperfections of this world. We have been expelled from Paradise, and now must live in a world in which death and the opposites hold sway. Through our own choice, we have rejected the perfection of oneness and sought out the separative life of the ego, and our internal psychological state is reflected in our external environment.

However, there is more. Let us now consider a question which atheists such as Stephen Fry do not appear to have contemplated. What is this world actually for?

There is an answer to that question and I will give it in a moment, first of all in words that the Masters used and then in my own words. But before I do I will ask another question which has a bearing on the answer to the first. What are we? What is a human being? Are we just the mind and body that are at the forefront of our immediate experience or are these just the outer parts, the sheaths, if you like, that cover what we truly are, being but the expression of that true self, enabling it to experience the material realm? I would say that only a mind overly influenced by worldliness can reject the strong probability, supported by many traditional teachings as well as by our deepest intuitions, that we are spiritual beings or souls that are using the mind and body as vehicles. These are part of us, but only the phenomenal part. However, we identify with them because we are in the material octave, and that is the cause of our confusion. It is because those in the materialist camp cannot see beyond their materialism that they cannot understand that this world is not intended to be a perfect environment for the embodied self. It is meant to facilitate that self to transcend its limitations. It is not a holiday resort but a training ground.

So, to quote the Masters, **Earth is a school**. That is what it is for and we are here to learn. To learn what we truly are, and to grow the spiritual seed that is within us through the various tests and experiences we undergo here. This material Earth is an arena for the development of consciousness, and we come here to learn and to grow. Growing can be painful, especially if the shell we surround ourselves with has to be broken open in order that we may expand out of our current limitations. But it is also liberating, and it is what we want whether we know it in our conscious minds or not. As a Master said to me, and this applies to us all so his words are something to hold on to in times of trouble, **"I can assure you that you wish this training to take place however difficult it may sometimes seem."**

As a platform for growth, this Earth must include scope for tests and trials as well as contain opposites, the tension between which can stimulate new growth and help us to avoid stagnation. And is it not the case that it is often only through a degree of suffering that we are jolted out of complacency and self-centredness, and more able to enter compassionately into the sufferings of others? Perhaps it is because Stephen Fry has suffered himself that he feels so strongly that suffering is something we should be concerned about and try to relieve. Of course, not all suffering can be regarded as potentially creative and an impetus to change, but some is and it should be clear that a life without a negative side to it is a life in which growth is much less likely to take place.

As for the suffering that may seem to have no creative purpose, we can turn for explanation to the idea of karma. Certainly this requires a belief in the pre-existence of the soul, and so will not be acceptable to everyone, but, if we are looking for something that reconciles the apparent contradictions of a benevolent God and an imperfect world, the law that we reap what we sow bridges that gap very well. So the imperfections we meet in this world are frequently the reflections of our own imperfections. That is not to say that the sufferings of the innocent can be blithely dismissed as their own fault. They may well be the result of previous actions, but they may also be restrictions accepted by the soul in order for it to grow, or even sacrifices it has volunteered to make to help alleviate world karma or arouse compassion in others.

Let us conclude with a brief summing up.

The purpose of this world is not in and for itself but as a school in which consciousness may grow, moving from an unconscious state to a self-conscious one and then on to god-consciousness. That is why it must be an environment in which work, effort and potential for sacrifice are required. Without these there can be no spiritual growth. The world is not perfect in order that we may become so.

The Truth About Suffering

The modern attitude to suffering is that it is a great evil which should be eradicated, as far as that is possible. Our whole moral system today is more or less based on the premise that what leads to personal happiness is good, as long as it doesn't harm anyone else, and what causes suffering is always wrong. But what if suffering is actually the whole reason for life in this world? What if the fact of suffering does not disprove the idea of God but actually proves it?

To make sense of this, on the face of it, bizarre idea, we have to understand what we are and why we are here. And what we are is not what we appear to be. The self, as we know it, is a false thing. It is not our true being. At the very least, it has lost its proper centre. Now, if this is the case then what that self views as good or bad is not necessarily so. That is not to say that suffering is good and happiness is spiritually corrosive. But sometimes, viewed from above, that might very well be the case.

For the worldly self that we all identify with, and look to fulfil, is an artificial construction that obscures our real self. That true self is the soul, which is a spiritual being, and the fact is that suffering is often necessary to make us aware of this. It is what is required to detach us from our identification with the ego-self and realign us with reality. No suffering means spiritual stagnation, though that is not to say that suffering should be sought. That would be the ego trying to manipulate its own overthrow for its own ends. But if suffering comes and cannot be avoided, then it should be accepted and the lessons it brings learned. And there always are lessons to be learned, even if it is the ability to endure without complaint and so grow in patience and humility. There is always the possibility of removing our concern from our worldly self and its fears and desires, and fixing our thoughts on something greater which is the true source of our being.

Naturally this only relates to personal suffering. The suffering of others is never something we should observe without compassion or idly stand by and watch, though even then we have to understand that it may be necessary. We have to develop the spiritual discernment that will enable us to appreciate what is suffering sent to teach the soul, or teach us that we are the soul, and what is suffering caused by the wrong conditions that human beings have created on this planet ever since they lost their connection to the spiritual world.

So the soul, a spiritual being, is what we are and our task here is to remember our origins. The soul on its own level cannot suffer, certainly not as it can do in the material world where the conditions, specifically the sense of separation, exist to make that possible. This is the world of duality in which we are alone, cut off from the rest of life, and it is that which both helps us to grow and causes suffering. The two go together.

Hence, strange as it may seem, suffering is actually something for which we should be grateful to God. It takes a certain spiritual maturity to see this and, like all such doctrines, it can be misunderstood. Suffering is not good. It is an evil. We are right about that. But it is an evil out of which good may come. Very possibly in a world that hadn't fallen it would not have been necessary, but this one did fall and so it is required even if, as I have been assured, **all hardships now will be amply compensated for.** This is not easy to understand. Can it be true? Can the pain of this world really be seen in a light that explains it, still more justifies it? I think it can. Is it really so hard to accept that suffering has a purpose and that one day it will be seen as no more than a bad dream when the day dawns? Naturally, in order to accept that idea we have to come to terms with the fact that we are only half made in our current state. We are still being formed and it may be that when the new man is finally formed, his past travails will seem to him well worth while in the light of his present glory.

So the conclusion I draw is that the fact of suffering can be taken as proof of God's existence and of his purpose for us. When we identify ourselves exclusively with our material being, then suffering makes no sense. But when we start to see ourselves as visitors to this world, come to experience the lessons it has to offer, then we can see it in its true light. And this was surely what Jesus demonstrated by his life and death. He showed us that accepted suffering can be the way to redemption and self-transformation.

What this means is that suffering can only be understood in the context of religion. In fact, both Buddhism and Christianity could be said to revolve around suffering but they have different attitudes to it. Buddhism arose specifically from the attempt to understand and, if possible, go beyond suffering. That was Gautama's motive in leaving home and trying to understand life. The solution he found and taught was the cessation of desire. We suffer when we hold on to things, so letting go of desire, in particular the attachment to it, brings freedom from pain. You might go further back and say that it's the sense of separation that brings about suffering. If we were one with life we would be complete and nothing could be added to us or taken away from us. So suffering at root is, or comes from, separation. This is the Buddhist position.

That is all true but I want to look at suffering from a different, more Christian perspective here. I want to look at it in a practical sense, as a purifier and true agent of spirituality.

Today, when all the wisdom teachings of the past are readily available, there are many people presenting themselves as spiritually advanced, or even enlightened, on the basis of a certain amount of knowledge and experience. But I must tell you that a person may have all the spiritual understanding in the world but there is no real wisdom without suffering. You may talk of love and profess an awakened heart because you know this is how a spiritual person should be, but there is no possibility of real compassion without having known deep suffering. It is as the Masters have said. **In pain alone you get true values.** Pain is the gateway to eternal life because pain strips away falsehood and pretence. You can always tell a genuinely spiritual person by their face and expression. It is not constantly wreathed in smiles, telling us what a loving, open, joyous person they are. It is marked by sorrow. I don't mean that they walk around looking miserable. That is self-pity. But they have been through the fires and that is etched into their face, for it is suffering, and suffering alone, that cleanses the soul and stamps the heart with spiritual truth. Only pain patiently endured gives depth.

It is a perfectly natural impulse to wish to avoid suffering, and it is certainly a mistake to seek it out with the idea of gaining spiritual kudos, as certain ascetics used to do. But suffering that comes to us in the ordinary course of life, that is, in effect, God-given, that is unavoidable, we should use as an opportunity for self-transcendence. It comes to burn out the fires of ego. It is part of the sacrifice that makes holy, and it is only through such sacrifice that holiness is born in the individual. Only when forced to by pain can we truly begin to give up the self. This is the reality of living in a fallen world. Self has become corrupted and made itself into its own centre. Suffering is what de-centres the self, or does so if the "patient" reacts to it correctly by offering it up to God and using it as an opportunity to go beyond himself. If you can, you should even see it as a gift in that you are being given a chance to graduate to a higher spiritual state. You would not be given this gift if you were not thought equal to the task.

Now, none of this means that one should not respond to suffering in others, or even that one may not pray for one's own suffering to be alleviated. Suffering is not in any sense a good or desirable thing, even if it can be used as a creative thing. The rule must surely be that one does all one can to relieve suffering but if attempts to do this come to naught, then one must accept the reality of the situation without resentment or resistance. This is particularly so in cases where you are the one suffering. See it as a chance to go beyond your present state. Accept the will of God and submit to the experience, seeking to use it as a springboard to greater understanding, an understanding that comes from having lived something, not just known about it.

As I have said, this is a doctrine that can be misunderstood. The fact that suffering is what I have called an agent of spiritual purification does not mean that all suffering in this world is sent by God, and should just be left to run its course. Most of it probably comes from the fact that we live in a fallen, corrupted world in which human beings exploit each other, and fail to live in harmony with the truth. This sort of suffering we should not only seek to redress, but also be aware of how we might be adding to it. But there is also spiritual suffering, frequently, but not always, mental in focus, which we must learn to recognise. Thus we need to acquire discrimination as to what is suffering caused by man's inhumanity to man and what is suffering that comes as part of treading the spiritual path. Complications arise when the two become mixed, as they can do, and karmic suffering is another factor to take into account, suffering that may be the result of decisions that individuals or groups of individuals acting collectively have taken. But determining the meaning and probable inner causes of events that occur in life is all part of the process of developing spiritually. We cannot look at these matters in a simplistic way by saying that everything that comes about does so for a single reason. This is a complicated world, and we must avoid the temptation to reduce serious spiritual questions to elementary formulae that can be expressed in a quick and easy catchphrase. Nevertheless, for the spiritual aspirant, it is wise to regard any suffering that enters into your life as having a purpose. That doesn't mean that you just lie down and submit to it. It may have come to enable you to develop the strength to fight it. But you must learn what you can overcome and what you must accept, so a good rule would be that initially you seek to solve the problem it presents and, if you can't do that, then is the time for acceptance and submission to God's will, knowing that his will is always to our own long term advantage, even if it does not seem like that from our current limited perspective.

It is a fact that the greatest saints appear to have known the greatest suffering, and we also have the example of the suffering of Christ before us, showing us that this is indeed the way to eternal life. And how could it not be, given that the barrier to eternal life is the fallen self or ego whose roots have become so deeply embedded in the soil of our being that we mistakenly regard it to be what we really are? But then, to put all this talk of suffering in perspective, we see what it leads to. The risen Christ, who has found his identity in God and is thereby released from bondage in form, which bondage is the cause of all suffering. So suffering is no more, gone, impossible. Its pain has been transformed into love. For note that form, as the expression of spirit, and its opposite pole in manifestation, remains. The risen Christ still has a body, but that now exists as the means to express goodness, truth and beauty. Its power to limit and its ability to be hurt are gone. Now it exists only to reveal the glory of the Lord, and to manifest the perfection of love. And, believe it or not, it is suffering that has made this possible. That is not to justify suffering but to explain its presence because understanding it will diminish the ferocity of its sting.

I am not saying that the risen soul can no longer suffer. This is a deep mystery, but I would say that such a soul can no longer suffer personally but can do so as part of the whole of creation. All is one, and the higher the soul, the more it is identified with the totality of life. Creation is still groaning to be fully born and perhaps until it is even God, in some sense, suffers but this is a suffering that in no way contradicts heavenly joy. It is the suffering of love.

I want to conclude this section with a brief consideration of the doctrine of the Fall since it is the Fall that is said to be the origin of suffering in this world, both human and animal, as well as the disruption in the natural world. The idea is that this world was created perfect but fell into imperfection because of an act of disobedience on the part of early man, prompted by a demonic interference.

At one time I thought that the Fall was all part of the general pattern of the evolution of consciousness, and that we had to know duality (the separation of subject and object) fully in order to transcend it consciously. Early man was unconsciously one with life. We had to fall into self-consciousness and know separation in order to rise, eventually, to a fully conscious union. I still think that. It's quite obvious really.

But, at the same time, did we have to know duality to the extreme extent that we do? I rather doubt it. So now it's not the descent into duality that I think was the result of our disobedience (or spiritual mistake) but the absolute separation that we feel from God. I can envisage a process where we still learned to be full individuals but without the degree of pain, suffering and fear of death that we have now. It would have been a kinder, gentler process, still fully effective but less of a long, hard slog. Less scarred by suffering and death. Also, it's clear that Nature has been deeply corrupted by something more than just the results of the misuse of human free will. That is why the Gnostics could think (incorrectly) that matter was evil in itself, and not the creation of the good God. The created world is good but it has been damaged right to the bottom by an anti-spiritual force, and so have we.

So I do think that a fall was part of the plan of human unfoldment and the growth of souls to true spiritual consciousness, but not the Fall as we actually experienced it which was the intended natural fall carried further and brought lower because of the demonic desire to corrupt God's creation, coupled with man's misuse of free will. If you want to know why there is suffering, look to the Fall.

Spiritual but not Religious

It is sometimes claimed today that spirituality and religion are two quite different things, with the former deriving from an inner experience of God while the latter is just a matter of externals, of doctrines and dogmas and obedience to authority. Spirituality is the understanding of an essential oneness between Creator and created, or even just of life, but with religion there is always a sense of separation between human beings and God. One is free, while the other has to do with law and custom. One is inclusive but the other is divisive. This attitude strikes me as focusing entirely on the virtues, or supposed virtues, of one and the defects of the other, and more than a little unfair. The truth is rather subtler than such a rigid distinction between the two would imply.

It is true that real spirituality goes way beyond religion of the elementary variety, that of the believer who believes what he is told to by the priests and conventions of his faith, and doesn't make much attempt to see further than that. He is satisfied with accepting outer authority and doesn't try to internalise the teachings. However, real religion also goes beyond this. Some of the most spiritual human beings on the planet have been some of the most religious people and, until a century or so ago, hardly anybody would have thought themselves spiritual who was not religious. So I would say it is not religion that is the problem but the mistaking of its outer form for its inner substance. Admittedly, that is not uncommon but it is not religion's fault so much as that of some of its leaders and many of its followers. The fact is we need both religion and spirituality. The one to provide form and structure and discipline and true doctrine, and the other to breathe the breath of life into that form.

It is indisputable that the moment a divine revelation starts to be codified it becomes subject to human interpretation, and its essential purity is lost. But this is true of anything which is translated from a higher level to a lower. Does it mean that we should never seek to express an intuitive insight in thought or word? The fact that such an expression descends to a lower level than the original inspiration (giving form to something inevitably restricts it) doesn't mean we shouldn't make it. Only that we should remain aware that any attempt to describe what is beyond description is necessarily limited, and that it can never capture truth, only suggest it. It's a cliché to say that the map is not the territory, but a map can be a great help when you want to go somewhere, and it makes sense to get the best map you can.

We live in the world and must bring our spiritual impressions down here if we would share them, or even understand them ourselves. Inevitably much will be lost in the transition but if we didn't do this then how would we communicate anything? More importantly, what forms of guidance would there be for others who cannot yet access the spiritual realm themselves directly? And, let's face it, that's most of us. Besides, aren't the advocates of spirituality, rather than religion, doing just what they decry in religion every time they give a talk or write or say anything? They, too, are making the abstract concrete for the purposes of aiding others.

I don't deny that religion can, and often does, descend into rules and regulations, but that is when it falls into the hands of men without vision, bureaucrats of the soul. It exists primarily, though, as spiritual guidance, a means of reconnecting earthbound and fallen man with his source in God. It does not seek to replace that link unless it has become corrupted. It seeks to restore it.

There is another point worth considering here. Today much that is called spirituality leans towards self-indulgence for if religion can lapse into mere observance of outer rules and regulations so spirituality, or what is called that, can descend into seeking what pleases the self or makes you feel good.

Spirituality may offer a direct connection to the source, in theory, but what if you are not able to make that connection or not able to make a true connection? At least the principal religions are based on divine revelation, and they contain an experience and authority that goes beyond that of just one individual, having been honed and refined by many great saints and mystics over the years. They have been thoroughly road-tested. On the other hand, spirituality without religion can mean following an individual path with all the possibilities of illusion and error that implies; a path, moreover, without challenge or sacrifice that has as its object the fulfilment of desire. It can just be a search for experience, with the idea of self-transcendence, if it actually exists as an aim, reduced to a personal goal, with its moral aspect ignored.

Not long ago I read an interview with an actor who had been through extensive drug use, multiple sexual relations and the rest of a self-indulgent worldly lifestyle but had now rejected all that, settled down, married and found spirituality. What did he mean by spirituality though? He thought that traditional religion had been meeting a human need but there was too much bigotry in it, too much sexism, too much emphasis on sin and not enough on fulfilling human potential. He thought we were right to reject it on those scores but that our descent into secularism and materialism was not the answer. He now believed in a higher power which we needed to get in touch with in order to find true meaning and fulfilment in our lives.

But was this a real spiritual conversion or was it simply the story of someone who no longer found any pleasure in his old satisfactions so needed to look elsewhere for what he had found there? Was his interest in spirituality inspired by a burgeoning love of God and desire for truth or did he want that higher power on his own terms, while staying resolutely faithful to the values of this world, which couldn't be questioned in his eyes? It was apparent that for him spirit had to accommodate itself to this world, God to Man. The notion that it should be the other way around did not appear to occur to him. Secular liberal values could not be challenged.

For a number of people nowadays "spirituality" is a lifestyle choice which they want to add to their other worldly possessions. It's an addition to their self-image, adopted for purely personal reasons. Tell them that it means you have to take up the cross and, like the rich young man, they will walk away. Tell them it means you must sacrifice and renounce the world, the flesh and the devil and they will look at you blankly or else laugh. They want heaven while staying firmly in this world. They don't see that the two are mutually exclusive. I know some might say that this is a start but truth is unlikely to grow from such shallow roots. The reality is, there can be no spirituality without a full and complete repentance. It needs more than a jaded appetite or a desire for higher consciousness. In a sense, you must be sick of the world and sick of yourself, too.

I wondered if this person acknowledged the wisdom of the supposedly archaic Ten Commandments? Did he see through and renounce the sins of the sexual revolution? Did he accept the reality of evil and see its power in the world? You see, just as some old-fashioned Bible thumping enthusiasts could focus too much on sin and not enough on love, so the modern spiritual but not religious person can focus too much on love, horizontally understood (i.e. not love of God, which is the only real basis for love of one's neighbour) and not at all on sin, unless that is understood as sin against fashionable, worldly values. He sees spirituality as something waiting there for him to take and make him feel happier as he is now, and does not understand that it is something that requires a radical transformation on his part, and that sin is just a word for what holds one back from that and cuts one off from true spiritual connection. He might be willing to engage in some kind of technique to get what he wants, but he doesn't see that techniques belong to this world and can never get you out of it into a real spiritual sensibility. They might work on a physical or psychological level. They can never work on a spiritual one. That depends entirely on motive, on what a man thinks in his heart.

The fact is that modern spirituality of the spiritual but not religious variety has no place for God, not the living God who is a Person, who has a will and a purpose. It might give him a token acknowledgement but he is not absolutely central, and he must be if spirituality is to be real and not dissipate into self-centredness and triviality. If we ask why God is *persona non grata* in so much spirituality of today, the answer seems to be that the acceptance of God would mean you had to acknowledge something greater than yourself which was real, not vague like an unidentified higher power waiting at your beck and call. Something to which you had to incline yourself and give yourself up to, holding nothing back. You could not have spirituality as an extension of your own personality. You would have to sacrifice that personality in order to have spirituality.

Then there is the point that spirituality is inclusive but religion divides. Yes it does. It divides truth from falsehood and greater truth from lesser. Christ did not come to bring peace but a sword. The unity promised by spirituality without religion is the unity of blandness and lack of discrimination as in proper discernment. It is a unity that denies quality and ignores the fact that God may be in everything but he is not revealed in everything equally.

Perhaps the most extreme version of the spirituality without religion idea is the belief that it is valid practice to use drugs to access spiritual states. But is the point of the spiritual life to access higher states or is it to acquire virtue? Drugs are an artificial means to try to take the kingdom of heaven by storm and therefore it is a fundamentally irreligious thing to do to use them. It is putting your will above God's. If God wants you to experience transcendent states, he is perfectly capable of giving them to you. However, he knows the strong likelihood that a person gets attached to these states and loses the reason for being on the spiritual path in the first place: that being to get closer to God through the heart not by means of any external technique or artificial aid. The use of drugs never made anyone a better person and actually belongs to our evolutionary pre-rational past, coming from a time when connection to perceived oneness was being lost and people sought to recapture it. So it is essentially degenerate behaviour. It is not a spiritual practice because it is valuing God's gifts above God himself. Can you imagine any of the saints doing this? Can you imagine Jesus or the Buddha recommending it? If you trespass where you have not earned the right to be, you will not be able to understand where you are. Only when you have earned the right of entry by the inner quality of your being can you respond to higher levels properly and in terms of what they really are. Spiritually speaking, you cannot separate knowing and being, and if you try to circumvent that rule you risk inner disconnection. This is acknowledged by all proper teachers.

Despite what I have written here, I myself have never been able to subscribe to any particular religion, and this for two reasons. Firstly, it appears likely that all religions are in a state of decline, and have been for some time. They are past their prime, and the fire lit by their original spark is dying out with the consequence that their ability to inspire and enlighten is greatly diminished. Religions are not eternal but follow the same pattern of birth, development, maturity, old age and death as everything else. So all religions, as they exist today, have lost the connection to the world of spirit they once had. Make no mistake, they did once have this connection, but the further they travel in time from their origin, the more they become embedded in this world and lose it, though they can be given fresh life now and then by an infusion of saints and true mystics. But the law of entropy still applies. There is always a balance between spirit and matter, life and form, in any true religion and when, as inevitably happens as time goes by, that balance becomes weighted too heavily on the side of the form and structure of the religion then it becomes more of a belief system than a pathway to God.

Secondly, I do actually agree with the statement that spirituality is a higher form of religion, since spirituality, truly considered and lived, is the reality of which religion is only a presentation in the lower worlds. Religion, in this respect, is a crutch which we must eventually throw away if we are to walk unaided. The point is, though, that to throw away our crutches before we can walk unaided is foolishness at best and arrogance at worst, and if you believe you can walk when you can't, you are likely to fall flat on your face. With that thought, here's something the Masters said on the subject of traditions and conventions that, with a little alteration, seems to me to be appropriate to our present subject. They told me that, **"conventions and traditions have their place in the world, some good, some not so good but still valid at some level, and, whilst most of them would be outgrown in time, they should be understood before they were rejected."**

So it is with religion. We may need to go beyond it to find truth in its fullness, but it exists to help us get to the point where we are able to go beyond it. To reject it before we have got to that point risks leaving us floundering in a spirituality of egotism. But, at the same time, to hold onto it in its outer aspects after a certain point shows an inability to distinguish between a lantern and its light. At the end of the day, religion only exists to serve spirituality. But spirituality without religion can very easily descend into self-indulgence and illusion. We need to be sure we have learned the lessons of religion before we can be justified in thinking we can do better without it.

Christianity and Immanence

One of the reasons that religion is at a low ebb in the modern Western world is that Christianity at some point lost a sense of the immanence of God. It lost the sense of spirit, leaving the divine as a remote, transcendent being far removed from this Earth. As a result, Christianity came to be seen by many as a religion of dry theory and restrictive morality. Indeed, in some respects that's what it became. At the same time, for people in the West, nature lost the sacred quality it had had in pagan religions and was emptied of meaning because Christians, always sensitive to the problems of pantheism, did not sufficiently appreciate that, while nature is not sacred in itself, it can be regarded as such insofar as it is God's creation and imbued with his being. Then came the scientific revolution which finished what that process had begun and stripped the natural world of any remaining mystique.

So Christians lost sight of a living spirit in nature and in themselves, and saw God as only out there. They created a radical duality between man and God with little possibility of bridging that gap, certainly not in this world. This left the field open for pretenders to the spiritual throne from Romanticism in the 19th century (also a reaction against the darkening of the imagination by science and the destruction of nature by the industrial revolution) to the various New Age religions in the 20th. But these lacked the moral centre that Christianity provided and, worse, tended to see the spiritual path as the deification of fallen or natural man, rather than the sanctification of the risen soul in God. They sought the spiritual by bringing the divine down to Man, instead of going the correct way of raising Man up to the divine.

This leaves people in the West with a problem. They can remain Christians, but with a religion that has lost much of its spiritual fire. They can take to Eastern religions, but I have never seen any real evidence that these work for modern Westerners. Or they can just adopt the materialistic sophistries of the day, which is what the majority of people do, since most people follow the crowd in these matters. None of these options are very satisfactory though some are worse than others, of course. So, what to do?

Human consciousness in the main has evolved to the point at which individuals have to make their own decisions. I said above that most people follow the crowd in terms of a world view and so they do just as they did in the past when most were Christians, ostensibly so at least, but those who are serious about finding a spiritual path now have to work out for themselves how to go about it. To be sure, one can just join a religion and go along with its practices and beliefs, fitting them neatly into worldly life just as it is lived by everybody else, and not letting them make any real difference to who or what you are other than in a vague and generalised way. But if you are truly serious about trying to discover the reality of the spiritual world and coordinate yourself to that, then you must find a way that corresponds to the deepest yearnings you have inside you, though always making sure that you are following universal spiritual truths rather than wishful thinking. That's not necessarily easy, but I believe that if you use the image of Christ as a yardstick and submit any spiritual approach to that, then you will not go far wrong.

For Christ is the spiritual template. He is the true image of the divine, not the only one but the truest one. And so, for the contemporary Western person, the spiritual path does still require taking Christ as the ideal and exemplar. Now, I don't think that means you have to become a Christian in the conventional sense. I feel that all forms of Christianity today are diminished and lacking the inspirational and transformative power they once had. If you don't feel that, fine, but if, like me, you do, then don't make the mistake of forgoing Christ simply because Christianity might often have become too enmeshed in the snares of this world and concerned with ideas, both religious and social, that did not seem so important to Christ when he walked the shores of the Sea of Galilee. Go back to his teachings as recorded in the Gospels and, most importantly, try to awaken the light of Christ within yourself. Christ must be born in you before you can even begin to think of yourself as anything other than spiritually asleep, and that truth is the same yesterday, today and forever.

You might wonder what I actually mean when I say that Christ must be born in you. Am I speaking purely symbolically and referring to something you could just as easily call Brahman or the Buddha nature or do I literally mean a connection to the real Christ? A bit of both really. I see Christ as the true personification, the real face, of an inner spiritual reality that had been intuited by great spiritual figures of the past, but was not fully revealed until 2,000 years ago in Bethlehem. Once the revelation has been made, that is what we should focus on and incline ourselves to, though this does not mean that those who, for whatever reason, don't do this but are still faithful to the inner truth of which Jesus Christ is the embodiment will be penalised. I would never say that only Christians can come to God, for that would be to mistake the letter for the spirit. However, I do think that Christ is the inner truth behind the highest and best of all religions, and the spiritual gateway through which all must eventually pass if they wish to gain eternal life. He is the divine prototype.

And so we come back to the truth that was lost by Christianity, or maybe just never properly acknowledged, that we are all sons and daughters of the Most High, put on this Earth to become more godlike. To be sure, we are all sinners but we are also gods in the making. Yes, we all err in following our own self-centred wills instead of God's but within us there is a spark of the divine fire, and once we become aware of this, and fan that spark into a flame through proper spiritual practice, then we will do greater things than Jesus ever did. He himself has told us so.

Eastern Religion for Western People

I wrote in the previous chapter that I had never seen Eastern religions particularly benefiting Westerners. That is a rather sweeping statement but, generally speaking, I think it is true, though, as with any rule, there will always be exceptions. Before proceeding any further, I should say that I have learned an enormous amount from Eastern religions, especially Hinduism and Buddhism, but I have learned this as an outsider looking in. I have never been tempted to adopt an Eastern approach, but I have used insights gained from studying these philosophies to deepen my own understanding of spiritual matters. So I am certainly not saying that Westerners should not study Eastern religions. I don't say they must, but I think that if they do, they will gain a lot thereby. However, studying a religion and fully participating in it are two rather different things. It is the latter I am referring to when I say that I don't think Eastern religions particularly benefit Westerners.

There are two issues here and I will get one of them out of the way quickly. Each religion has its own mythology and really you cannot adopt this. It has to be part of you, and that is definitely the case where Hinduism is concerned. I do think you have to be Indian to be a Hindu. Traditionally that is the case anyway. You might feel you can take the philosophical aspect and leave the mythical side alone but then you will remain outside the religion as a whole, so your interaction with it will always be somewhat artificial. It will be like reading a poem in translation. Of course, you can get something from it, but you are not reading the real poem. Where Buddhism is concerned, the situation is a little different as that is not so tied to a particular place (Hinduism is the one major religion that comes from the spirit of a land rather than an individual prophet or founder) but it is still soaked in a mythology and garb that will always be alien to a Westerner.

They might be able to access the intellectual spirit of the religion but the form will not be natural to them, and this is more important than it might appear. The spirit is certainly the main thing but the form houses and earths that spirit so cannot just be dismissed. In a way, it and it alone gives true access to what you might call the living kernel of the spirit. The appearance of something cannot be completely separated from what it is inside, not without damaging the whole, which then becomes less effective. It's like body and soul, each needs the other to be complete.

I'm not saying that nobody can be converted to a religion in which they have not been born. That's clearly nonsense. But the gulf between the modern Western mind-set and the ancient Eastern religious attitude and view of the world is too wide for there ever to be a genuine and natural union between the two. The meeting will always be at several removes, so adopting a religion that comes from long ago and far away, and is not "in the blood", will always have a certain artificiality to it and that means that it cannot ever really be a natural thing, which it must be if it is to spiritually feed and nourish the soul as it should.

But even supposing this bridge can be crossed, there is another problem. Most Western people who look to the East for enlightenment are doing just that. They are looking for enlightenment. They are aspiring mystics seeking a higher state of consciousness. It doesn't matter if you say that Nirvana or Brahman is beyond a mere state of consciousness, that is basically what these people are doing. They seek mystical experience. But is mystical experience, or even enlightenment, what the religious path is really meant to be about? Is it to do with tracing life back to its unmanifest source of consciousness in itself or is it to do with making the soul fit to receive divine grace, thus rendering it holy, which requires that it acts out of love for the divine being rather than desire for any condition or state of mind or being, spiritual or otherwise? You might think these are just different ways of describing the same thing, but there is an important real difference between them and it is to do with motive as well as goal. In the one, individuality is renounced, or even rejected, for what you might almost call an ambition, but in the other it is brought to perfection by being taken beyond itself in love. Love is key, and to know the Creator in love is the true spiritual end and purpose of the soul. Only this takes us beyond the separate self with its selfish goals.

Many Western people who take to Eastern forms of spirituality are on the run from the idea of God, and have a human-centric approach to spirituality, privileging knowledge over love. But you will only find the true God (and there are many states and conditions you might mistake for God in the higher planes if you are not pure of heart) when your approach is fully theocentric and your motive is love of the divine. If you seek knowledge only, as in enlightenment, you may well find a spiritual state that seems profound, but you will not be granted the Beatific Vision which is a stage beyond Nirvana, defining that as simple entry into timeless being. God gave you the gift of yourself. Don't refuse that gift or throw it away. Give it back to him, purified in love.

I lived in India for several years. I met many serious and sincere seekers while I was there, and yet in only a minority of them did I see a real spirituality, by which I mean that the search for enlightenment was almost always the underlying motive. Consequently their concern was invariably with God Immanent rather than God Transcendent, so it basically amounted to a quest for the spirituality of experience rather than one of self-sacrifice in love. Of course, some sort of God was often acknowledged but not in the sense that he was actually real, and the true goal of the spiritual search. Not in the sense that he was the Creator and the Father, and the purpose was to reach a proper relationship of love with him. Sometimes he was even something to be gone beyond by the real mystic, who was expected to leave him behind in the relative world when he penetrated to the non-dualistic reality behind all things. So the conception of God had changed from the Christian idea that he was the whole reason for the spiritual search, and its only proper end and purpose, to putting him in a more peripheral place where, even if he existed, he was no longer the prime focus. That was now deep within themselves. God was within them as their truest self, but there was not the full appreciation that this true self within them actually had its origin outside them. They had lost the real sense of God, and forgotten that for us he is transcendent before he is immanent because he is the Creator. As a result, they were approaching spirituality with the idea of gaining something from it rather than, as should be the case, giving something, namely yourself.

Ancient Eastern philosophies are wise and profound. They have much to teach us, and I believe that some of their practices can help anyone develop spiritually and start to align himself with the soul within. But what they offer the Westerner is mainly to do with knowledge, technique and method, and true religion does require more than this. To go beyond the ground of universal consciousness to God as he is in himself, not as he might be in the aspect of pure being, we need love. The prime teacher and exemplar of love is Christ. He is what he teaches, and the only way we can become that is to become like him. Christ is still all important for the West.

The Buddha brought light to the world but Christ went further. He included all that the Buddha brought of light and the wisdom of oneness but added to that divine love which, be it noted, is only acquired through suffering. The Buddha, the paragon of the East, sought to escape suffering but Christ, through his acceptance of suffering, transformed it into a path to divine love. It is Christ who set the spiritual pattern for the West to follow.

No One Comes to the Father Except Through Me

This is an extraordinary saying which addresses something many people interested in esoteric or mystical forms of spirituality tend to shy away from. But it's something that we, especially we in the West, must always come back to. Is Jesus Christ a spiritual teacher or is he the spiritual teacher?

"No one comes to the Father except through me." Can these words possibly be true? On the face of it they seem to be saying that Christianity is the only valid spiritual path. But do they really mean that or are they pointing to something different? Remember that at the time they were spoken there was no such thing as Christianity. There was Christ, but not yet a religion based on his teachings. Let me set forth here what I think Jesus meant by these words.

To begin with, though, there is little point in even considering this matter unless you think that the words might be true, and that Jesus had, and still has, the right to say them. So let me say straightaway that I do think they are true. When we come across them in the Gospel of St John, we don't say to ourselves that here is a megalomaniac with severe delusions of grandeur. Such is the power of Jesus's personality, the strength of his aura, you might say, that we take them seriously. We believe them. I believe them. They don't make me want to give the person who says them a wide berth, and yet, if I heard them from anyone else, I would certainly react like that, even from great saints and sages. In the context of the one who speaks them, these words convey a deep sense of truth. It is just as it says in the Bible. Jesus speaks as one having authority.

But even if we accept this saying as true, there are still various ways in which we can take it. We can interpret it literally or metaphorically, or we can say that it is true on both these levels.

I think this last way is the correct way, and that it is true in both a literal and metaphorical sense. No one can reach God who does not go through Christ. However, to say that does not mean that everybody must become a Christian. We must distinguish between outer and inner truths or paths, and also between the incarnated Jesus in whose name a religion was founded and the risen Christ who, on the heavenly plane, is the Master of Masters and the Teacher of Angels and Men. Not that these are different beings. It is more that they are the human and divine faces of the same being. The risen Christ is the inner channel through which we all must approach God, and though this does not negate or replace the individual connection we all have to God, who is eternally present as the core of our being, it is nonetheless the way through which that individual connection is opened. We all have the divine spark within us but that spark can only be fully ignited through the inner spiritual reality that is Christ, through whom we must pass in order to find God the Father.

Not everyone will be able to accept this as an intellectual proposition and, from the perspective of an outer spiritual practice, not everyone needs to. Many who do not follow Christ outwardly may be doing so inwardly, in that they follow the essence of the teachings he embodied. In the same way, many who follow him outwardly may not be doing so inwardly. Christ does not have a monopoly on all forms of the teachings that lead eventually to the Father, Divine Reality, but he is their personification, their instantiation, and they are given life and salvific power through him.

So, the outer sense of these words may not apply literally to everyone but the inner sense does, and so does the metaphorical sense, and what that means is this. Those who seek God only as an impersonal force, who restrict him to a kind of universal cosmic consciousness or One Life, are misconceiving the nature of reality. God the Father can only be known through God the Son means that the hidden mysteries of God can only be accessed through an acceptance of the personal nature of being. I AM the Way, the Truth and the Life. No one comes to the Father except through ME. You cannot dismiss the concrete and the personal and fix your spiritual sights solely on a nebulous abstract. Why? Because only the personal allows for a genuine love and humility and proper sense of one's place in the divine chain of being. You cannot know the Father, the Universal Absolute, without acknowledging the Son, the Particular. You cannot find truth except through love. That is the metaphorical sense of this saying but it does not reduce the significance of the literal interpretation, in its inner form, one jot. Both are true.

On several occasions here, I have argued against the idea, basic to Advaita Vedanta and Buddhism, that the personal belongs to a lower level of reality than the impersonal and is therefore, in some sense, unreal. I have said that the Personal God is not merely a limited expression of Impersonal Being but intrinsic to existence at its deepest level. Christ teaches us that ultimate reality, the Father, cannot just be pure, unqualified, featureless being or the Logos, the Son, could never be. God cannot just be life. He must be alive. Deeper levels of reality must include what derives from them, and so, if the highest reality is conceived of as above our understanding of the personal, that can only mean it includes the personal in perhaps a similar way that a cube includes a square. The square does not reduce to nothing at the cube level. If that is what is meant by impersonal I have no argument with the term, but normally that is not what is meant. The square is dismissed altogether, reduced to, as the Buddhists say, emptiness. Ultimate being, or the Father, may be beyond the personal as we normally conceive it, but it is impersonal only to the extent that God is not limited by or to form, again as we conceive it. But even if, in his essence, he is beyond our idea of a person, he is not less than a person. He is not mere abstraction but real in the most concrete of ways. He is "I" always, forever and eternally. As he tells us of himself, "I am that I am." Therefore, for us, made in his image, which means reflecting his reality, God must be personal before he is transpersonal. And this is the metaphorical meaning behind the words spoken by Jesus who is the portal to and human face of the Father.

Christ, Spirituality and the West

After nearly 40 years of interest in spiritual matters it's increasingly clear to me that any genuine revival of spirituality in the West must be linked to Christ. The huge range of spiritual approaches that opened up in the 20th century, particularly since the 1960s, has led many to believe that all paths to God are more or less equally valid and it's just a matter of choosing the one that suits you best, whether that be a form of Eastern philosophy, Western esotericism, paganism, occultism, New Age mysticism or whatever it might be. All roads lead to Rome, so to speak. And it's true that most of these systems can help lift a person out of the materialistic morass into which humanity has fallen over the last hundred years, and give him or her a grounding in spiritual understanding and practice. But in all of them something important is missing, and that is Christ. For the fact is that Christ really is the light of the world. He is the spiritual truth that transcends all others, and any form of spirituality without him will always risk falling short. I speak for the West here. I don't say Christ is irrelevant for the East but it has built up its own way and tradition, and the outer form of Christianity, as it currently stands, is a Western one. Eastern approaches to God are certainly valid on their own terms even if, as I firmly believe, they do not contain the fullness of truth that those centred on Christ do.

You might ask why a real spiritual renewal should be linked to Christ. Why can one not follow one of the many spiritual paths that do not involve a recognition of Christ as Son of God, and still find a way to the goal? First of all, I would say that depends on what the goal might be. Enlightenment, liberation? These are imported concepts and not part of the Western spiritual tradition which is focused on the sanctification of the soul in union with God, the transcending by the soul of itself in humility and love.

But then I would ask a question in return. Why are you failing to recognise the primacy of Christ? What is it in you that rejects this? For a heart that is really open to truth should recognise that Christ is the greatest spiritual light that has yet appeared on this Earth. In his person he brought together and went beyond all other forms of truth. This was symbolised by the attendance of the three Magi at his birth. For, let us remember, they were not Jews, demonstrating the universal nature of Christ. If you don't see this, you should look again, perhaps with misgivings caused by the failings of earthly forms of Christianity set to one side. If Christ is in your heart then you will recognise him. If he is not then he needs to be because he is the door through which we all must pass on our way to God. Not necessarily in his outer, revealed form but through his inner reality, yes.

But to answer the question posed in the previous paragraph more directly. Any spiritual renewal in the West must be focused on Christ because only Christ safeguards us from the excesses of pride and illusion, those twin perils of the spiritual path. By humbly submitting oneself to him, and walking in his light, one is protected from all the falseness that surrounds spirituality, and there is a lot, as any experienced spiritual director will tell you. But there is another reason, implied earlier, and wonderfully simple. It is that Christianity, in its essence, is true. Since Christ arrived in the world, all other spiritual approaches are subordinate to him. However effective they might have been in earlier times, they are now secondary, having been superseded by him, and the reality is that if you ignore this you are ignoring something fundamental to spiritual truth. A higher form of it has been presented. If you don't respond to that you are missing a basic spiritual fact, which means that either your powers of intuition are lacking or something in you is suppressing them for reasons of its own. Consequently, your spiritual progress will be held back from reaching its proper potential.

One of the important aspects of a Christ centred approach

to spirituality is that it fully recognises the personhood of God. In this day and age a featureless divine life is very attractive to many, possibly because it does not challenge us as much as the recognition that we have a Creator to whom we owe not just our being but also our love. Giving what we owe is actually our true fulfilment, and to some this is a wonderfully liberating idea. But others find it oppressive and reject it. That is their right, and yet human nature is such that we can only really confess our sins (and hence be forgiven and find redemption) to a personal being. And without full repentance and acknowledgement of all our erring ways, it is almost impossible for the self to transcend itself. The renunciation of ego, which is what I am talking about here, can only truly be done in love not knowledge. Love means a personal God. That is what this book is all about.

What I have said here does not mean that any renewal has to be centred on the Christian churches or one of the current outer Christian structures. This is actually something of a problem at the present time because what the world needs now is not so much Christians as followers of Christ, and we might usefully distinguish between the two. Most modern Christians are very influenced by the ways of this world, their Christianity having often adapted itself to worldliness. Besides which, Christianity itself could be said, like all religions, to be approaching its best before date due to natural processes of inner decay and outer change. To put it bluntly, modern Christianity is sometimes an imperfect representation of spiritual truth. Despite its many qualities, it has areas of weakness, particularly when it comes to an understanding of consciousness and its transformation. Consequently, many of the more spiritually sensitive souls will nowadays choose to be spiritual freelancers. This has its corresponding difficulties in that personal experience might become the focus of their spiritual approach, and that can lead to problems unless checked and balanced by a higher understanding. So we need to tread with care, and this is why it is important for anyone on the path, whether as a member of a spiritual community or as what I have called a spiritual freelancer, to have the image of Christ stamped on their heart. That image will act as a light to keep you safely on the spiritual straight and narrow. Without it you are more than likely to stray and, while there are certainly other images, there are none so deeply effective and true.

The principal point I am making here is that even if a modern spiritual seeker cannot accept Christianity as it exists in any of its contemporary forms, and I understand that, being in a similar position myself, this is no reason to reject Christ or to reduce him to simply an enlightened soul like any other. He remains the Way, the Truth and the Life, and any spiritual revival must take that into account if it is to be properly effective. It may encompass other things, but that must be central. Outer Christianity may not be the force it once was but Christ is eternal. An image that comes to mind here is that of a fruit which contains the seeds of its own regrowth. Thus Christianity, as we have known it, cannot perhaps be revived to its past glory and spiritual creativity, but its renewal will come from the seeds left behind by those.

One of the ways modern Christianity has fallen short is that it has shown an insufficient appreciation of spirituality. A strange thing to say you might think, but what I mean is this: Christianity has neglected the immanence of creation. It has lost touch with the reality of a divine presence in nature and in man, and any revival must be far more in tune with the essential mystery, poetry and magic of life than recent Christianity has been. Thus it must be consistent with the understanding that the spirit of God is present in creation, and that he is not just the transcendent Creator but also immanent being. But again, he is not just immanent being but our loving Father too, and all these things must be taken into account, with none left out, or you will have a limited and incomplete spiritual approach that leaves you outside the full reality of God.

It may be that those who predict that the next age will be dedicated to the Holy Spirit, the spirit of truth within us all, are right. This was the idea of Joachim de Fiore in the Middle Ages who theorised that the ages of the Father and the Son would be followed by one of a more universal spirituality. But each age has to be built on the last, and if it rejects the past it has no foundation and will fall. Thus whether the next age is that of the Holy Spirit or not, the fact remains that this inner spirit can never be known without full acknowledgement of the Father and the Son. The idea of the Holy Spirit without the Father and the Son is a snare for the unwise. This is another reason for the necessity of any future spiritual revival to be grounded in Christ.

Who is this Book For?

Some of the ideas expressed in this book might be seen as too influenced by the New Age for most Christians, and too Christian for many people interested in more modern forms of spirituality. In the same way, they could be regarded as too influenced by Eastern spirituality by orthodox Christians, and too focused on Christ by those of a Hindu or Buddhist persuasion. So who am I writing for?

What I hope is that there are enough people like me, who might have searched in various places for spiritual understanding, as those of the last few generations have had the opportunity to do, and then come back to Christianity, though in a somewhat unorthodox form, viewing it differently than if they had never left it. The Christianity of my childhood was largely an external thing. God was presented as out there, and the idea that he was within never really got a serious look in. It was beneath the surface if you looked but it was never brought out and explored in any depth. Nor were there any religious instructors, or so it seemed, capable of doing this. Investigation of Eastern mysticism and various forms of alternative spirituality, including Western esotericism, helped give people an insight into the sense of immanence; the reality that God is not just the seemingly remote Creator out there but also exists within us as our very self, and, through proper spiritual practice, we can access something of this reality. Many people have made that journey over the past fifty years or so. Through meditation and other ways, a substantial number of people from all faiths and none have explored the idea that within the human being there is a deep connection to divine truth, and, by going beyond conventional identification with the mind/self, we can enter into a living communion with the one life that pervades all manifested being.

But the idea of God Immanent needs to be balanced by the understanding that God is also the Creator who exists independently of (though not separately from) us. So we can be one with God but we are never hierarchically equivalent to him. Without a full sense of this our spiritual search can easily descend into a subtle form of narcissism and, even if it avoids that pitfall, it remains incomplete as, I believe, the understanding of Buddhists and others who do not acknowledge God, and neglect the possibility of a relationship with him, does. For spiritual reality presents itself to us in two ways, and to know it properly and correspond to it correctly we must understand it in its totality. In one sense it might be conceived of non-theistically, as the Buddhists do, but in another and more profound way, it is theistic, and God's purpose is that we come to know him as a Person, having a relationship of love, and do not just rest satisfied with the frankly static existence that is pure being when separated from becoming. We grow and grow, everlastingly so, and he does, too, through us. This is the true goal of existence. Not to abandon becoming for being, but to combine the two in a full and joyful awareness. And only in this way can we really become truly spiritual, both in our understanding and in our person, our character.

But there is more and this has to do with Christ. For Christ is not just a righteous teacher or enlightened soul in the Hindu or Buddhist sense. He is the Son of God, come to this Earth to offer salvation to those who would accept it. That is traditional Christian teaching, but what does it mean exactly? First of all, the Son of God? Sometimes this is revised nowadays and interpreted to mean that he is a human being who has realised his oneness with God. We are all sons of God in this sense. He just knows it. I think that's true, but it by no means covers everything that Christ is. In a way I can't fully explain but intuitively see as true, Christ is the archetype of this, the divine pattern, which we can copy, but only because he is there to enable us to do that. An exemplar and a template. So our sonship, which does exist, is only able to be activated through and because of his. He is what you might call the Universal Son of God, the Cosmic Christ, the only begotten Son in whose spiritual life we can partake and so become like him. But without him our sonship could never take full effect. He is the central fire through contact with which we, when we have made ourselves combustible by conforming ourselves to truth, can catch flame ourselves.

At one time, I might have not properly appreciated this, and gone along with the common modern belief that Christ was a forerunner and simply someone who had realised his divine nature ahead (well ahead!) of the majority. But this belief, while no doubt pleasing to a democratic sensibility, no longer seems tenable to me, if indeed it ever really did. It may be that those who distinguish between the man Jesus and the spiritual being Christ, who overshadowed Jesus from the Baptism onwards, are onto something, and in that case this spiritual being would be the divine prototype or Logos in that he embodies the principle that is the Son of God. And Jesus the man would perhaps be the first of the human race to attain Christ consciousness. But this is a heretical notion, dismissed by Christianity, and anyway it only pushes the sense of Christ as the only begotten Son of God back a bit. It does not alter the reality that Christ is *the* Son of God who must be born in us before we too can become proper sons and daughters of God.

Where does that leave those sincere spiritual people who, whether because of birth or cultural tradition or for whatever reason, do not accept this premise? I must stress sincere because I think that those who actively reject Christ are leaving themselves open to the other fellow. But naturally there are other valid spiritual paths. God provides access to himself by various means. Ultimately, though, these must coincide with the inner truth of Christ to be successful, and I have no doubt that the most open channel to spiritual truth, the one that best and most clearly reveals divine reality, is through the person of Christ. You might call him the fact of which others are the image or the symbol. They can be very true and accurate images or symbols but he is the fact.

Which brings us to salvation. What is that? To understand this, we have to come to terms with the idea of the Fall. That is, human beings in the distant past lost their connection to God, probably unconscious or automatic at the time, and began to follow the path of their own selves. This cut them off from the rest of life and locked them in their own minds, which may have had certain benefits but also brought about the disastrous alienation we know today. Salvation is the return to God, and this, it seems, was only made possible in the fullest extent by the incarnation of Jesus. To save us from the downward spiral into materialism and spiritual darkness, to save us from ourselves in fact, we have to recognise the reality of Jesus. This means recognise him *as* reality. Mere mental acknowledgement of this is not sufficient. The heart must open to accept Christ within itself, and this is the second birth. It is the turning away from self and back towards God, and that is salvation. When we have accepted Christ as reality (or a spiritual equivalent which carries something of his inner nature and being) then we are saved, but that is a beginning not an end. The acceptance of Christ must be the first step that leads to the transformation into Christ, and this is what most forms of Christianity have either not emphasised enough or missed out altogether. It is why so many people have found Christianity lacking and looked elsewhere for spiritual sustenance.

Therefore we need first of all to see the truth in Christ and see Christ as the truth. But then we need to become that truth ourselves, and this is what the spiritual path is meant to accomplish. Most serious Christians have taken the first step, but that really is just the first step, and there is a good long journey to go on after that to transform an ordinary human being into a fully conscious son or daughter of God. I would like to think I am writing for people who are making that journey, as I hope I am doing myself, people who understand that Christ came not only to save souls and turn them back to the light, but to show them the way to transform their very being into that light.

Meeting The Masters Revisited and Revised

When I wrote my earlier book, my primary aim was to recount the story of my experiences with the spiritual beings who had instructed me. I thought the fact of their existence and what they had to say might be of interest to many people frustrated by the dead end of modernism. I sought to present this in the context of the best of Western and Eastern, as well as theistic and non-theistic, spiritual approaches in order to arrive at a more universal perspective that reconciled these by focusing on their higher, unifying essence. I realised these weren't fully reconcilable but possibly at the time I didn't fully appreciate the extent of the differences between them.

The main part of that book still stands. The strictly factual part that describes my encounter with the Masters, their words and their teachings and my reactions as a spiritual apprentice is what it was. However, my metaphysical understanding has changed a little, and if I wrote the book now I would put the more theoretical parts in a slightly different way, with less emphasis on the identity of mystical traditions and more on what I consider to be the deeper truths revealed through Christ. Thus I would place the non-dualistic and Buddhist points of view, which are more or less the same, at a different level of truth to the idea I have been describing which sees the destiny of the soul as to be made one with God, in a union in which individual identity is transformed but retained rather than rejected in favour of an unqualified pure consciousness without difference admitted in any way. I would lay greater stress on the love of God as the supreme spiritual path, with knowledge, as in the perception that the soul and divine ground are one reality, as an incomplete approach that does not lead to the fulfilment of our true purpose. I would put a conscious union with God at a higher level than self-sufficient identity with the uncreated part of one's being.

And I would further stress that the aim of the spiritual disciple should not be enlightenment but the sanctification of the soul, achievable only through the grace of God which grace can only be properly received and merited after lengthy purification of the fallen self.

As a matter of fact, most of this was already plainly implied in the book as, for instance, in the passage about the absence of God in Buddhism or comments about there being a duality beyond non-duality. I also mentioned that the Masters were more like wise abbots of a Christian monastery than present day teachers of enlightenment, which was a word they never used. However, it was not spelled out quite as unequivocally as it might have been as I wished to be more inclusive in my approach at the time, and was also less clear in my own mind about the difference between the impersonal absolute as the ground of being and the Creator God. Coming to an understanding of the meaning of the Trinity as the ultimate truth of things has helped clarify matters for me, particularly as to how oneness and difference can be completely reconciled in a higher union in God with no loss to either. It does seem that only a Trinitarian metaphysics, or something like it, can really account for reality as it is and do no violence to the integrity of either the One or the Many, either the uncreated source of all or creation.

I once assumed that all mystical traditions described pretty much the same thing, which was the union of the soul with God. They just put this in different ways, depending on where they were coming from. Because my spiritual training was with the Masters, as described in the book, I refracted everything through that prism, and didn't pay sufficient attention to the fact that different traditions do actually say different things and have different goals. I read books about the various religions and studied some of the writings of the great mystics and philosophers, both ancient and modern, but tended to assume that any differences were at the level of expression only. I now see that they are not all describing the same thing, and that some do have a more restricted point of view than others. Also, some come from human attempts to know truth while others have revelation from above at their core.

As the Masters never told me what to think from a philosophical or theological perspective, but focused entirely on practical instruction, I did not take my metaphysics directly from them. They were only concerned with inner change and development and did not point me towards any outer spiritual teachings, letting me sort that out for myself. However, their words and their presence definitely point to a certain form of truth, and that is the form in which love and humility are the primary spiritual virtues; indeed one in which virtue itself rather than knowledge is the primary spiritual quality. And true virtue only comes from one place, that is aligning oneself with the will of God. So the Masters demonstrated the full truth of the transformation of the individual soul into a divine union with God. Think of us as messengers from God, they said. And so they were. Ceaselessly active on his behalf. There was no question of them resting in some state of blissful inactivity which an unqualified non-dualistic reality would necessarily imply. If there is no reality in creation, why bother with it? I am aware of the two levels of truth theory (absolute and relative) each with its own place in the scheme of things, but see this as evading the question as to whether creation, and therefore us, is really real or not when full spiritual awakening dawns. It does not properly answer the crucial question as to whether we, as individual souls, endure. The revelation of Christ shows us that we do.

I don't reject anything I wrote in the book, which is first and foremost about my experience with the Masters, but I feel that my theological understanding has become more nuanced now. Strangely enough, it has become so since being challenged by non-dualists after an article of mine (The Non-Duality Trap) was put on a non-duality website. This led me to consider the implications of pure non-duality more deeply, which made me realise that my assumptions about it were incorrect. It is quite dissimilar to Christian mysticism. Its rejection of God and the individual are, I now believe, deeply flawed for reasons I have given at various points in this book.

So what I am saying is that, *pace* Buddhism and Advaita, individuality is important. The Masters have certainly transcended identification with the limited individual aspect of their being, as they are one with God, who is the centre of their lives, but individuality remains. In fact, it is more developed than it is in most of us, who, in comparison, are only half-formed individuals. A heaven of identikit saints would be a sort of hell, wouldn't it?

Most of all, what I would now insist on is the reality of God. This might seem a strange thing to say when talking about spiritual matters. But increasingly I have noticed the tendency in present day approaches to spirituality to downgrade God's presence in the picture, whether as a lesser reality than pure absolute being or as not existing in any true form at all. This is a very great error. God exists and he exists in a personal form, though I am not saying he is restricted to that. God will always remain a mystery in his essence. Nevertheless, God as Person is absolutely real, for personhood is not a limitation on being as erroneously thought by the non-dualists. It is at the very centre of reality. God cannot be limited in any way but to envision him as an abstraction of pure being seems to me to be much more of a limitation than to say he is a Person. And without this personal side, nothing really has meaning as it is the personal that give life its savour and joy. This is why modernism, which is founded on the active denial of God, is basically anti-life. It is, in fact, nothing less than a death cult. That's the truth.

To say that God is a person does not mean he is an object to us, something or someone "out there". That could never be, for he is the essence of personhood, the "I" behind all "I"ness, the archetypal Person from whom we borrow our person-ness or individuality which is given to us from him and reflects his. Thus we meet him not as an object but as the eternal Subject, the root "I" of our "I". But he has created this world in which the one and the many co-exist like harmony and melody in music and if we are to encompass the fullness of reality we must take both into account.

So the only parts of my earlier book that I would amend now are those that imply that God as Person is somehow lower or less real than the Impersonal Absolute. I always struggled with this intuitively. If that were the case then where did the original "I" come from in the first place, what was love, what was goodness, why were the Masters so individual and why did they speak of higher Masters, i.e. point to a hierarchy even in heaven? Moreover, it was not a teaching the Masters themselves ever gave. However, the weight of metaphysical authority, particularly that of the East, appeared to affirm it, and it can be seen as just an extreme form of the fact of oneness. But an understanding of the nature of the Trinity, seeing how there is difference even at the deepest level of unity, has given a better metaphysical foundation for my intuitive sense of how things are.

There is perhaps one minor point I should clear up. When the Masters said that one should forget the personal self and merge with the universal self, this might appear to support the idea of abandoning the sense of being an individual and becoming one with the absolute. In a way it does, but it does not mean giving up individuality. As I have said, the Masters themselves were full individuals. The only difficulty here is on a verbal level, a common problem when discussing metaphysical matters. Personal can refer to the reality of the person and this was an idea that the Masters fully endorsed. They demonstrated the truth of it. However, it can also refer to the personality in the sense of the separate rather than individual self, me and mine rather than I, and it is this idea of himself as a separate being that the disciple is asked to renounce. *Not* the idea of himself as an individual. God created us as individuals because it makes things much more interesting for him, and he does not demand suicide but self-transcendence. Forget the personal self does not mean deny you are an individual, but don't exclusively identify with your individuality. Know yourself to be a spark of the divine, fully one with your Creator.

Incidentally, in case of misunderstanding, I am not saying here that our approach to God should only be on a personal level, and that the practices and attitudes associated with a formless or apophatic approach to truth are invalid. I believe that each should be balanced by the other for a comprehensive understanding, just as love should be balanced with wisdom. The Masters counselled both prayer and meditation for the disciple, and this points to the need to take a twofold attitude to the spiritual path, attending to the divine reality in both its transcendent and immanent aspects. Either on its own is incomplete, even if the truth is that the ultimate aim of God is that he may have a personal relationship with us, and that we may become gods ourselves. He did not create souls merely for them to be reabsorbed back into his being, eternally resting in the darkness of the Godhead as though they had never been. He did so in order that they might add to the glory of creation through multiplication of oneness and joyous communion between all parts of it. He is a giver not a taker.

The Inadequacy of Official Christianity

Although I have spoken of my belief in the universal truth of Christ, and also criticised the spiritual but not religious approach as largely unstructured and insubstantial, I have also mentioned that I do not belong to any established church, or any spiritual organisation at all for that matter, and never have. My view is that we are living in that time known as the Kali Yuga in Hindu philosophy, or the latter days in Christian eschatology, and it is a time of spiritual decline during which all outer forms of spirituality, including those religions which have previously promoted and protected truth, are falling away from the purity of their original vision. But that is not the only problem, for while these avenues to truth were more than sufficient to satisfy man's spiritual needs in the past, they all arose at a time when human consciousness was rather different to what it is now so they can no longer perform their function so effectively.

I once asked the Masters about official religion. The religion in question was Catholicism, which I actually think is the religion that has preserved a good deal more of spiritual truth than most.

I asked a Master if it was wrong of me to try to ease Michael away from the Catholic Church, given its authoritarian structure and refusal to acknowledge any truth it did not itself contain. He replied that he had told me before to trust my instinct. He said that the Catholic Church, like any outward form of religion, was good for souls on a certain level but it was time to lead Michael away from it into a new and higher understanding of life. He told me not to be intolerant but to do this with love and patience.

I realise that's quite enough for the Masters to be damned as demons in some quarters but that is to misunderstand their words. The key phrase is "outward form of religion". We all at some stage need to transfer our attention from the outer path to the inner path, and that often means going beyond conventional religion which, in the language of Orthodox Christianity, is more concerned with salvation than theosis. But theosis, which is the sanctification of the soul, the making of the soul godlike, is what the spiritual path is really all about. We do not just need to be believers in Christ but become Christ-like ourselves and for this, religion, outer religion of any sort but in particular that of the modern churches, can sometimes be almost as much of a hindrance as a help.

That is my first point but my chief complaint against the modern churches is that they have all, some more than others but all without exception, allowed themselves to be corrupted by "this world". Far too often they now conceive of spirituality horizontally, which means that their eyes are fixed on human beings rather than God. I suspect this is part of a demonic attempt to undermine truth, but it is aided and abetted by the feeble quality of church leaders who, for the most part, are not men of vision, still less saints or mystics, but administrators and bureaucrats, more concerned with their organisation than divine truth. The result has been they have conceded more and more ground to the modernist ideology of worldly progress, and now have values little different from the current left/liberal ethos which is founded on the centrality of the human being as he appears to be in this world. This is a process that has been ongoing for well over a century, but has really picked up speed over the last two or three decades.

The result is that much official Christianity is now a hollowed-out shell. It has followed the world instead of renouncing it. It has succumbed to the temptation of appearing loving rather than actually being loving, and this it has done because it has misconceived love, restricting it to a kind of non-judgmental egalitarianism and due to the worldly personality rather than, principally, the spiritual soul. Tolerance, currently meaning full acceptance of pretty much anything regardless of what it is, has become more important to it than truth. That has inevitably led to a loss of truth and a disconnect from the transcendent God with the result that many churches now seem more concerned with matters of social justice than spiritual transformation. And all this has come about because contemporary Christianity has made the huge mistake of trying to compromise with the modern world.

Many branches of Christianity have followed that path and effectively despiritualised themselves. They have become absorbed into the modern anti-spiritual mind-set because they were not strong enough to resist it. The spirituality of the leaders and members of these branches of religion has been too shallow, too insubstantial and too little felt for them to be able to shake off the influences of this world. Consequently they have accommodated themselves to it, become part of it and are now not only indistinguishable from it but actively fight on its side and against real religion, if by that we mean, as we should, spiritual truth.

They have been led astray by the zeitgeist of the present age and the propaganda emanating from all aspects of society, the media, education and the intelligentsia in general who all plough the same furrow of metaphysical ignorance. And what is this furrow? It is the rejection of a transcendent absolute and the restriction of reality to this world, and of humanity, too, as it appears to be in this world. And that has led to the ideology of liberalism which is the defining doctrine of the modern age.

It is important to realise that liberalism is an ideology. It is not based on any kind of reality but on a false perception of reality resulting from the eradication of God and the preference for abstract theory over truth. It also fundamentally misconceives human nature by ignoring the fact that, while human beings may originally have been created as good, we are all now corrupted by sin, that is to say, an innate selfishness. This may be an unpleasant truth but it is still a truth and to ignore it leads to illusion and worse. Whatever the benefits of liberalism as a reforming corrective to an established order that has allowed abuses or when decadence has set in (and it does have a validity in that context) it should never become, in its own right, a replacement for an established order based on the reality of God and the truth of religion. But that is exactly what has happened over the last hundred years or so. Liberalism, as the currently favoured moral philosophy of atheistic materialism, has become accepted truth, and to oppose its premises is to deny goodness. That is why compromise is so tempting. Who wants to be thought a bad person? The problem is that liberalism does not lead to real goodness but a kind of by the book goodness which, of course, is not goodness at all. This is because it produces a conformist ideologically based mentality, opposed to any sort of real individuality which is necessarily non-egalitarian.

Official Christianity has compromised. The trouble with compromise is that it tends to assume truth lies between two extremes. But does truth lie between the extremes of right and wrong? Does it lie between God and no God, between truth and a lie? Evidently not, but when a lie is powerful enough, and almost universally accepted, it can take on the mantle of a truth. The only thing to do then is to reject it and point out its falseness. You cannot make a compromise with it or you will be infected by it and the infection will spread, eventually taking over completely. This is what has happened in the Western world, which has more or less set the agenda for everywhere else.

The churches have compromised but do we, as spiritual aspirants, have to? Well, we live in the modern world and so, however spiritually misguided it is, we do have to compromise with it to an extent. But we also have to stand out against it or else we run the risk of becoming defined and, worse, defiled by it ourselves. Even if we have to go along with it externally some of the time, we must make sure that our hearts and our minds stay free and are not co-opted into submission to its dictates. How best to do this? By seeking outer and inner support, the former through spiritual reading and companionship, if we can find it, and the latter through prayer and remembrance of God. Jesus warned us (in Matthew 10:22) that those who followed him in spirit and in truth (not just nominally like many modern-day Christians) would be hated by everyone but, if they endured to the end, they would be saved. Here is both a test and an opportunity and what it means is this. Don't compromise with what you feel inside to be true, however much it may conflict with commonly accepted wisdom. There's no need to be confrontational but be true to what you believe. Stick to your instincts. Clever words and arguments can always be spun to make instinctive feelings appear foolish or wrong but these should be ignored, though they can be helpful in that they can sometimes show up gaps in instinctive perception or reveal what is prejudice and what really is instinct. But intellectual argument or debate cannot be regarded as primary, especially if it goes against basic intuition. God has given us a mind in the heart which goes beyond all else. Stay faithful to that.

If you want to reassert intuition over liberal ideology, even when that appears rational and logical which it often does in the restricted context of this world and within the framework that it itself has set up, then you must go back to basic principles. Basic principle number one is the reality of God. You must start from that. It is fundamental. But then you should go further and reject the egalitarianism of liberalism for the very good reason that this reduces humanity from a qualitative (spiritual) to a quantitative (material) level. It also flies in the face of a common-sense perception of reality. **Men are by no means equal on the earth plane** said the Masters. Men are different, men and women are different and, while that is certainly not a cause for dismissing anybody, it does mean that intrinsic qualities are important and should be acknowledged. We live in a quantitative age. Diversity is allowed, and even encouraged (probably as a way to eradicate quality) but only on the basis that all diversities are equal. If we are all the product of material forces working blindly to no end or purpose, then maybe we are all equal, all equally pointless, meaningless and valueless. But if we are individual souls created by God who, through our own endeavours and the function of our own free will, are working our way towards full spiritual understanding and expression, then, at any one moment in time, we are very far from equal. Individuals, cultures, even nations will all have made greater or less progress towards that end.

There is another point to add. You may wish to avoid compromise but nevertheless be forced into it because of the language and terms in which any discussion is framed. For if you express yourself using the language and terms of the modern world, as is difficult not to do, you are defeated before you start since these carry certain inbuilt assumptions. Language determines how you think. This is why revolutions attempt to change language before anything else. So avoid human rights and stick to justice and mercy, forget democracy and choice as arbiters of how things should be and propose instead proper authority (divine and natural) and objective truth as yardsticks. Don't discuss or think in terms of sexism, racism, feminism or any other -ism, but in the context of goodness, truth, love and spiritual unfoldment as seen in the light of a divine Creator. This is reality, the rest is ideological theory which may intersect with reality at certain points but deviates from it at many more. Bear in mind that if you express yourself using the vocabulary of the reigning liberal ideology in an attempt to expose its flaws, you will fail and probably end up looking like an ignorant bigot. By and large, official Christianity has failed to do all these things.

Compromise is often necessary in the case of day to day life. But when it comes to truth it must be resisted, especially now, in this time of universal spiritual decline and demonic attempts to subvert reality. Unfortunately the churches have not proved equal to the task. They have succumbed to the shallow half-truths of this world and lost connection to transcendence. Too many church leaders have taken their direction from outer things and ignored inner truths which, even when acknowledged, are frequently seen in the light of theories based on worldly or materialistic priorities. Instead of rejecting the world, as all spiritual people must do, they have surrendered to it.

Christianity and Salvation

I've been thinking about the idea that anyone who believes in God and accepts Christ as his or her saviour goes to heaven. Is this really the case? Does it not matter how you believe and the extent to which you apply that belief to your life? Does it not matter how much you reflect the reality of Christ in your own being? It surely must do or else why bother to be a saint? You might as well just believe in your outer mind and carry on as normal, not overtly sinning but not really doing anything very differently to anyone else either. That, of course, is precisely what many professed religious people do but it's nowhere near good enough and, on a certain level, is even hypocritical. For if spiritual belief does not translate into radical restructuring of the self, it is insipid and can hardly be called belief in the religious sense. To believe in God, if it is to mean anything, requires a different sort of belief to believing that the earth goes around the sun, which doesn't demand a response. For if belief in God does not become absolutely central to everything, what sort of belief is it? After all, as James says in his second epistle, when talking about the necessity of both faith and works for salvation, even the demons believe in the one God.

While sincere belief in God and Christ (or another valid religion) may be sufficient to pass some kind of earthly examination, it is not sufficient to get an individual to heaven in the true sense of what that means. This is where we must make the crucial distinction between salvation and theosis. The former is just the first step on the road to the latter which is divinisation of the human soul, and what we are put on earth to achieve. For we are not just called on to believe in Christ but to become Christ-like, true sons and daughters of God, ourselves. We may already be this in potential but that potential must be realised, and for this to happen a lot more than simple belief is required, even if simple belief is the first and necessary step.

It might help if we could see that the higher worlds are not just made up of heaven and hell (however we conceive these) but that there are many different levels of being, becoming progressively more spiritual the closer we approach to God. By that I mean that greater vistas of light, love, beauty and consciousness open up the higher we ascend but we must have developed something that corresponds to these in our own being. So the ordinary believer will find himself in a spiritual realm that approximates to his own inner development. If this is limited so will that be, whatever his beliefs might be. The saint will find himself or herself in a truly heavenly world because he or she has fully purified the soul. By the same token, someone whose spiritual consciousness is darkened or closed will find himself in a similar environment, one that reflects his own darkened state. Then again, souls at different spiritual degrees of development could function on the same level but perceive that differently according to their transparency to God.

All of which makes the idea that mere belief in God is enough to go to heaven far too simplistic. For one thing, there is no "heaven" as such because "my Father's house has many mansions", but, for another, it is how that belief transforms you that matters, not the belief itself which falls into the necessary but not sufficient category. Belief must act like the leaven in bread. If it doesn't have a transformative effect, then it's no good and the soul will not rise.

Belief in Christ might point you in the right direction but until Christ is born in your heart you are a worldly person. I am not talking about the extravagant melodrama of being "born again". This may or may not be a spiritual thing. More often than not it is a purely emotional reaction, a religious excitement of the feelings, not a true spiritual awakening, and one that will wear off as the emotion passes. But when the light of Christ is actually born in the heart then you start the transformation from earthly personality to spiritual soul, and it is only this that makes a person a true Christian. Belief is part of it but until belief becomes absorbed in the heart, and is not just an intellectual acceptance of a theoretical proposition, it will not take you very far.

Here are some quotations from Jesus that bear this out and tell us that merely believing in him is insufficient. He calls us to something far more radical than that.

- Many are called but few are chosen.
- If anyone would come after me, let him deny himself and take up his cross and follow me. For whoever would save his life will lose it, but whoever loses his life for my sake will find it.
- Unless your righteousness exceeds that of the scribes and Pharisees, you will never enter the kingdom of heaven.
- Strait is the gate, and narrow is the way, which leadeth unto life, and few there be that find it.
- Many will say to me on that day, "Lord, Lord, did we not prophesy in your name and in your name drive out demons and in your name perform many miracles?" Then I will announce to them, "I never knew you! Depart from me, you lawbreakers!"

It's difficult to take from these sayings of Jesus the idea that belief in him is all it takes to get to heaven. For one thing, what sort of Christ are we believing in? The true Christ or a concoction of our own or someone else's? The fact is that to believe in the true Christ, you have to have his image in your heart already. You have to have the spiritual capacity to respond to reality. Naturally this doesn't have to be very highly developed at the start. Its development is what the spiritual path is all about. But it has to be there in some sense. You must respond to the real Christ and not just an image, sentimental, made up or whatever, that you have got from somewhere external. So yes, belief in Christ will no doubt get you to heaven but it must be the true Christ as he is known in the heart, and you must act on that belief.

Christ exists within us all but we can only really begin to know him when we step out of ourselves and the worldly mind, and engage with existence intuitively. Belief is like getting down on the starting line. You have yet to run the race.

The Spiritual Decay of the West

The whole ideology of the modern West, and increasingly the East as it falls under the shadow of the West, is built on the denial of God. Sometimes we try to convince ourselves that this is a rational response to the world as we see it but that is just not true. There is no proof, as science sees proof, of God but there never has been. Indeed, there never could be because, by definition, God is outside the realm of material science. He is not a physical thing and cannot be such because something cannot be the creator of itself. No, the truth is that we do not want there to be a God because we do not want our freedom, as we see it, to be in any way curtailed. We are against God because we are for ourselves. It is not wrong to be for ourselves but these selves should be seen in the context of something greater which is their real origin.

It is clear from history that human beings have often rejected God in an attempt to be free but this freedom is merely that of the human ego and so is just another and deeper form of bondage. Moreover, the nature of the human being is such that when you have no God to worship, you look for something else as a substitute to satisfy that need which is the need for self-transcendence. Now we have taken to all sorts of false ideologies and beliefs in order to do this, but they all prove hollow and insubstantial because their roots are not in truth. And, strangely enough, we actually know this but cannot bring ourselves to accept the conclusion, so we persist in our fantasies. We construct belief systems that pretend that man is primarily a social being or a sexual being or a political being or whatever else it may be, and we base our attitudes on that. But man is first and foremost a spiritual being. Everything else springs from this. If that is denied or ignored the result will be that we live a lie and our hearts and minds will not conform to each other. There will be an alienation caused by this split which will only deepen, the wider the split becomes. This is the situation we find ourselves in today.

Modern man has gone mad and doesn't recognise his madness, which increases by the day, with the result that he needs to build more and more elaborate houses of cards, in science, politics, the arts, even certain forms of spirituality, to hide the reality from himself of his rejection of truth. This resembles nothing so much as an adolescent rebellion, and we are indeed like the prodigal son when he was at his furthest distance from his father. The question is, will we, like him, eventually repent and turn back or will we carry on our self-indulgent ways to their inevitable conclusion? This question can be posed both individually and collectively. There's not much we can do about the latter but the former is of crucial importance, and the answer is entirely up to us. The good news is that wherever we are, we can start to turn around now. From this very minute. Nothing can stop us except our own lack of will.

This chapter is called the spiritual decay of the West but one cannot say with any certainty that the decay started at such and such a date. There has practically always been an eroding of spiritual truth, even if it is restored from time to time. But perhaps one can date the start of the decay in its current form to the end of the Middle Ages when God began no longer to be viewed as at centre stage, and humanism became the predominating ethos. The creature started to take over from the Creator. This did bring advances in certain areas, and I don't doubt was divinely inspired, but against those advances we must set the fact that, as time went by, we lost the sense of truth as an absolute: an objective reality that stood above us and to which we should co-ordinate our being. We accepted the idea that reality depended on our interpretation of it and that, as a consequence, there was no such thing as reality. It became malleable. So our roots were in shifting sand. Is it any wonder we have become so restless and confused? How could we be otherwise, given the unspoken assumption that there is nothing real, nothing true, nothing absolute? Only the understanding that God is real can give our lives that fixed, immovable centre which we need to feel secure. Without it we are hollow men who can be blown about in any direction but never find peace.

Decay means that something that was healthy is rotting and normally this is a one-way process which cannot be reversed. However, in spiritual terms, it can if it receives (to put this in modern terms) some energy from outside the system. The birth of Christ was the supreme example of that. But, on a smaller scale, this can happen to each one of us individually if we open ourselves up to it, and that means (putting it this time in traditional terms) if we repent of our past ways and have faith. Faith in what, you might ask? How can I have faith in God if I don't even know what that means? I would say you don't have to know what it means. You just have to allow yourself to acknowledge the reality of a Creator who is all love and all goodness, and who is the source of all truth. I say, "allow yourself" because this is the reality and all that is preventing you from recognising that fact are the obstructions you put up with your self-centred thought and ego. That's all. Without your suspicious mind (which you are not asked to suspend but to see as something that interprets more than it perceives, perception being an instant thing, not taking place in time like mental processes) you would see the reality of God intuitively and then you could build on that. In this matter, it is the mind that blocks perception, though when it is correctly guided by intuition then it can help to deepen awareness and understanding.

Therefore, acknowledge the Creator. For people in the West the best way to do that remains the Christian way or, as some might prefer to think of it, the way of Christ. He is the Illuminator of the Way. For those who might not be comfortable with aligning themselves with a particular branch of Christianity, all somewhat diminished in modern times, Christ can still be the centre of their spiritual life as he is the human face of God and in his person transmits the essence of the divine. This is not a recommendation for a pick and mix approach to religion, but a recognition that while all religions, including Christianity, have lost much of their spiritual force in this day and age, Christ has not. He remains what he has always been, which is the Way, the Truth and the Life, though I mean this in a universal sense not a narrow sectarian one. Everybody, except perhaps the greatest saints, needs a form for their belief or it will prove weak and unsustainable. The form of Christ is the best because it embodies the truth beyond form to the highest and most perfect extent that has yet been known in this world. Christ can reverse decay.

A Meditation on Christmas

It has become an annual tradition to complain of the commercialisation of Christmas, and I am not going to do that here. After all, what's the point? We have gone so far down that particular road there can be no turning back. But Christmas has not only been commercialised. It has been thoroughly trivialised, too, with every year bringing a further reduction of the sense of what its meaning really is, to the extent that the Christian aspect is now almost an embarrassment. We are happy to talk about a generalised peace and goodwill to all men but only in a rather bland, humanist context. Reindeer and elves? Fine. The birth of Jesus? Not so good. It might be divisive. Even many religious leaders appear to have succumbed to this watering down of the Christmas message, so much are they a product of their times, seemingly unable to stand back from the relentless flow of materialistic assumptions which increasingly frame all our discourse, our language and what passes for our philosophy.

So here I would like to consider what the true meaning of Christmas is, and I will start off by saying that it has nothing to do with peace and goodwill. This may be a part of it but it is by no means central. Nor, for that matter, is love, another word that has been hijacked by people whose understanding of it seems to be limited to a general sense of benevolent tolerance. But love is not merely well-meaning egalitarianism. It is a spiritual quality that can only be correctly understood in a spiritual context, and it cannot be separated from truth. To be sure, the materialist can come up with an imitation of love but an imitation is what it will be, since real love derives from the soul. If the soul is denied then so is love, and all you are left with is a copy or reflection on a lower level, empty of any real substance, though possibly better than nothing.

What then is Christmas about if not peace and goodwill? The

answer to that is to be found in the image of the star shining in the winter night over Bethlehem, an image that is plainly symbolic, though not only symbolic, and speaks of something that combines a wonderful simplicity with great profundity. And what it tells us is that the message of Christmas is redemption from darkness. For Christmas is about the entry of supernatural light into the spiritual darkness of this world, and its core message is that those who recognise and follow this light can be saved from the darkness that constantly threatens to engulf us, a darkness so pervasive that it is not even recognised as such by many of us. Indeed, so successfully have true values been inverted today, that sometimes it is even mistaken for light.

So the true message of Christmas has to do with the salvation of the soul. The rest, peace, goodwill and so on, is peripheral to that central point. Now this means three things. First of all, it means we have a soul. An immortal part of us that is not derived from or determined by the body, or even the mind as normally considered, and which will survive death. Secondly, that soul requires salvation. It is not in a good state at the moment. It certainly needs to get somewhere other than where it currently is. And thirdly, salvation is possible. The light exists but we must acknowledge and accept this light. We must recognise it and allow it to illumine us for, though it may be supremely powerful, it is not coercive and will only come when invited. The most powerful thing in the universe enters this world as a weak, defenceless baby. What a teaching there is in that!

There are those who would like to rebrand Christmas as a pagan winter festival, a sort of eat, drink and be merry Saturnalia. And there is nothing wrong with that unless you think this is all there is to it. Being merry is an excellent thing, and eating and drinking are rather good, too. But tomorrow we die. What happens then? The entry of the light of Christ into this world tells us what may happen if we accept that light into our heart. This does not simply mean acknowledging with our mind that

Christ is the Lord or something of that nature. That is a purely external thing. There is a big difference between Christ as a person out there, and the light that he embodied. I am not saying the two are separate but the one informs the other not vice versa. It is this light that you must accept and strive to be illumined by if you would embrace the true spirit of Christmas. For Christ does not just want your mind, he wants your heart and soul. His desire is that we break out of the self-created prisons of our egos and join him in his heavenly kingdom. This will eventually require death and resurrection, but to begin with, the entrance to Christ's kingdom is through the heart and Christmas is the key that will unlock the door.

I do not think of myself as a conventional Christian in the external sense. As I have said, I am not a member of any church. However, my experiences with the Masters and my exploration of many spiritual traditions have never taken away my basic sense that it is in Christ that all teachings are consummated. I have always seen him as the supreme saviour of the world, and I feel that, though there are other valid spiritual paths, the light of God shines most brightly through the figure of Jesus Christ.

It is often said that all religions are one on the level of mystical experience and only separated by their dogmas and doctrines, which are ultimately outer things. That may be so but it does not mean that all religions are equally true. There is a fundamental impasse, for example, between Buddhism and Christianity in terms of how they view the Creator God, never mind the centrality of Christ in the scheme of things. I believe that the Christian view is the more correct one and comes from a higher revelation. Besides which, mystical experience is all very well but it really only points to the unity of consciousness on a supra-formal level, and entry into this state is not the primary goal of the spiritual life. It's clear from the teachings of the Masters, and many others, of course, that the purpose of the spiritual life is not the attainment of some state of supreme consciousness or enlightenment. It is the sanctification of the soul, fitting it, through repentance, purification, self-sacrifice and whatever else it takes, to receive the grace of God, thereby allowing the individual to enter a full and complete relationship with him, leading to deeper and deeper union. This truth is taught most effectively and revealed most clearly in the figure of Christ, and through the teachings of Christianity.

The nature of life, with its complexities amidst fundamental simplicity, equal significance of the One and the Many, essential balance and complementarity of sameness and difference, and importance of goodness, beauty and truth, is just what one would expect if at root it were a Trinity of Persons and not mere impersonal abstraction: subject, object and the relationship between them. This is just a fancy way of saying that God is Love. Only Christianity fully understands this. As a result, only Christianity really values the person, the individual and all that comes from the reality of the individual. Thus, to say, as we are wont to do nowadays, that all religions share the same universal values is not really true. Certainly, they share many values and agree that the spiritual is fundamental, but they do not agree on precisely what the spiritual is or on the true nature of the spiritual. Only Christianity fully accepts the personal nature of reality and because of that is able to see the purpose of Creation, explain the nature of evil, and understand the essential quality, reason for existence and goal of the human being. This is not to disparage any other religion, for all undoubtedly contain truth and offer guidance. But it is something worth pointing out at Christmas, at a time when the relevance of Christianity is being attacked by its opponents, misunderstood and trivialised by many of its exponents and forgotten by the rest of us.

When I was younger I sensed there was something unique about Christianity but was under the fashionable impression that all religions said more or less the same thing and were just different ways of bringing man to God if one practiced them seriously enough. I still think that is the case, within reason, but I also think that the salvific power of other religions was greatly augmented by the advent of Jesus Christ in this world and the spiritual impetus that advent gave to everything that could receive it. Thus it affected all genuine forms of spirituality and gave them a boost. It is no accident that the Mahayana form of Buddhism postdates Christ, and even Hinduism acquired extra spiritual force from Christ's arrival in this world and the spiritual power he released. This statement is clearly unprovable and would certainly be rejected by Hindus and Buddhists alike, but I make it because it seems to me to be the simple truth. It doesn't diminish other religions to say that they stand in the shadow of Christ. They remain what they are, which are vehicles given by God, or those that act on his behalf (since God delegates), to help souls in this world return to their source, but in them all there is still a veil over the fullness of truth. That veil was lifted by Christ. Other religions are effective in their own way but they are incomplete. Only in Christ is the truth made complete.

The World Today

It's sometimes difficult to tell if one's impressions are wholly objective or if there is a subjective element to them, too, but at the moment it really does seem as though the vice of materialism (pun intended) is growing ever tighter in our world.

The environment is actually becoming more like it is stated to be by science. Inner quality is withdrawing and consciousness is being constricted. The world is becoming harder and more solid. Don't you feel that?

At the same time, space is contracting, time is speeding up and distinctions are being erased. Differences between male and female, human and animal and even good and evil are all being diluted and broken down, and though there are corresponding reactions to this, reactions are what they mostly are. The general direction is towards uniformity. Everything seems to be being ground down to the undifferentiated state of prime matter.

It can never quite get to that state because that would be annihilation, but it can approach it and this is what spells the end of an age. Quality is replaced by quantity, and the digitalisation of information is a good example of that. This is clearly the most spiritually destructive thing there could be but it is happening and the speed at which it happens in all areas of life is increasing. What can we as individuals do about it?

To begin with, we can recognise that outwardly it is part of an inevitable cycle. That will save us a lot of grief. But then we must understand that inwardly it need not affect us. We can stay detached. We don't have to be swamped by the spiritual ignorance of our time. Indeed, that is the test of our time. We are summoned to remain faithful to the truth, even when the truth is trampled underfoot. This is not just an intellectual matter. It's a question of where the heart is. There are many people who adopt a spiritual worldview but don't make that primary in their life. It's an add-on to ordinary existence, which remains their basic focus. It is not transformative as it ought to be.

I am not talking about a religion. Lots of people do make their religion central but is it the outer form that is important to them or the real inner truth behind that form? Maybe it's a mixture of the two but we must make sure that the real motivation behind all we are and do is dedication to the inner truth. I doubt religion as we know it will exist in the heavenly worlds because it will not be necessary and we must try to have a mind that lives as though we were in those worlds now because in a certain sense we can only gain entry to them when we have the corresponding mental state. Like attracts like in the spiritual world absolutely, not just in the general sort of way it does here. I am certainly not dismissing religion, but ultimately it is a tool, not the real heart of the spiritual exercise.

If God does not exist there is no point to anything. That is not put forward as a reason to believe but it's a big indication that he does exist. The reality of meaning and purpose is demonstrated by the fact that their lack is so keenly felt. Not by everyone. The majority of people live in a state of distraction. But some people always, and most people sometimes, stand back from the superficialities of daily life to ponder on why, where and what. This is the voice of God calling you home. You should listen to it and seek to retrace that thread to its source.

We have to understand that our world is sunk in illusion, partly as a result of the increasing materialisation of the environment as time moves along from the beginning of an age to its conclusion, but this process is accentuated when our passive submission to the illusion reinforces it. We do partially create our own environment. If we, the collective we, imagine the world to be nothing but matter, then nothing but matter is what it starts to become. The environment actually grows denser to our perception, and more spiritually impenetrable. The outer reflects the inner, which then confirms the inner. The illusion starts to become real. But we are not obliged to accept this, and we must stand against it if we wish to be amongst the seeds that actually sprout and grow rather than those that fail to reach up towards the sun and perhaps even die.

The world today is in a parlous state because human beings have denied the fullness of their humanity, seeing themselves as animals ascended rather than spirits descended. We are of this world rather than visitors to it, or so we imagine. This has led us to reject the hierarchy of being and replace it with various false ideologies based on mistaken metaphysical concepts. If you don't know where you have come from, you won't know where you should be going. If you don't know what you are, you won't understand what you should be. But first the intellectuals of the world, seduced by the cleverness of their own minds, and then, following on from them, the ordinary people, have closed their hearts to what they are and where they come from. The thought form they have built up has become like a powerful elemental being which is actually turning this world into what they have imagined it to be: a solid, hard material world with nothing real beyond it. Even the discoveries of modern physics have not changed this, as they could have done, because they are too remote from our ordinary experience.

Nevertheless, as dark as this world might become, God is always there and the truth will eventually triumph. This we have been promised and it is impossible for it not to be the case, anyway. Therefore all we have to do is stand firm and hold the line. Manifest the truth and be a light in the darkness for those who may be looking for one, even if they don't know it. There will be many such, souls born into the spiritual ignorance of this contemporary world, who in their hearts cannot find any joy in it. They sense its falseness but cannot see in which direction lies truth because all their education and all their culture has denied it to them. The propaganda put out by "this world" is terribly strong. Be ready for them when they come your way, and know that in helping them you help the world, because you are helping in the fight against the hardening of the mind and the darkening of consciousness.

Perhaps you think this all sounds rather vague and abstract but it really boils down to the least vague and concrete thing there could be. God is real. He is present, here and now, and our task is to know him. Don't succumb to illusion and darkness. Open your eyes to truth.

Liberalism is the Materialisation of Spirituality

The next few chapters might be regarded as controversial when seen in the light of contemporary beliefs but my aim in them is to dig beneath conventional received opinion in the attempt to show it is built on unsound foundations. If current attitudes arise from a misunderstanding of what reality is, doesn't it make sense to point that out? So that's what I am trying to do but I realise it will not be perceived as such by people still in thrall to modern ideologies. I would just ask them to suspend judgment and try to respond without prejudice. What if we have taken a wrong turning and are basing our lives on a false view of the world, one that has forgotten the Creator and his purpose for creating?

The modern liberal position, which is pretty much the standard orthodoxy for Western educated people these days, can be seen as a materialistic distortion of spirituality. This is why it is hard to argue against from the perspective of a lack of belief in the Creator. It might make some kind of sense if there were no God. But then if you deny God you have literally no grounds for any kind of coherent understanding of life whatsoever. Consequently, you are forced to make things up to somehow fit in with your metaphysical ignorance.

The 20th century had the potential to be a time of spiritual rebirth. From the higher dimensions of life, forces rained down on humanity. New ideas were introduced onto the mental plane that were intended to carry us on to the next stage in spiritual growth, one in which the intellectual development of past centuries could be combined with a spiritual/intuitive outlook, and human beings could learn to integrate inner reality with outer.

Unfortunately, whether because of our own personal

weakness, the failure of our political leaders, artists and philosophers or because of demonic derailment (or most likely all of these) this did not work out as it might have done. Spiritual ideas were responded to but on a materialistic level and without acknowledgement of their true origin. Higher consciousness was interpreted in terms of lower consciousness. Even where spirituality was admitted, it was often from the perspective of the worldly self, with that as the driver instead of the passenger as is the proper course.

Thus the brotherhood of Man was recognised but not the Fatherhood of God. The complementarity of male and female was recognised but misconstrued as the sameness of equality. Condemning sinners was seen as wrong but so was condemning, or even recognising, sin. I could go on but it should be clear what I am driving at here. Ideas that were true on a spiritual plane were misapplied to the phenomenal one, and the real spiritual was either ignored or seen in the light of the material. By this I mean that what might have been true for the soul, as an unfallen spiritual being, was interpreted in the light of the fallen earthly self. The transcendent was brought down to the immanent.

This is why it can be hard to argue with someone of a liberal persuasion without seeming like an old-fashioned bigot. He thinks he is standing for goodness and truth, progress and enlightenment, ignoring the fact that if he is a materialist these concepts have zero meaning. But in his eyes, as far as they can have meaning, it is his ideology that best corresponds to them. And his ideology that has put right so many wrongs of the past. This is why so many people have unthinkingly adopted leftist attitudes and why those who oppose them are often forced into extremist positions, either real as in a compensatory over-reaction or apparent because they conflict with the unrecognised prejudices of liberalism. You don't believe in equality? You're a fascist. You think feminism misleads women and disrupts the natural relationship between the sexes? You're a sexist. You think mass immigration was a mistake? You're a racist. You think homosexuality is contrary to God's laws and means of expression? Etc, etc.

Part of the problem is that people responded to these new spiritual ideas from within the limitations of their already existing worldview, but that was not all. There were also demonic attempts to subvert and undermine truth, aided and abetted by their many servants in this world. A small minority of these consciously so, but most just able to be used and exploited because of their own rejection of God.

One of the principal ways this was achieved was through the sexual revolution, the unharnessing of sex from marriage. As all genuine spiritual teachers know, sex is such a powerful force that, if unconstrained, it takes over as the prime motivating factor in peoples' lives. Now it has not only been let loose but is artificially stimulated by fashion, music, art and general culture to extreme forms. Even people who may not participate so much in this, either through choice or lack of opportunity, still live in a world in which they are surrounded by sexual imagery and the attitude that anything goes as long as it doesn't hurt anyone else holds sway. But it is precisely because sex is a physical manifestation of a spiritual energy that its use purely as a means of pleasure is so detrimental to any kind of spiritual growth or development. Union between a man and a woman (and that, and that alone, is what sex is) must take place on as many levels as possible to be in harmony with spiritual truth and the wholeness of what a human being is. To restrict such a powerful force to the physical level alone, which is basically what the modern approach entails, will cut the individual off from the spiritual more effectively than practically anything else, especially when it is regarded as not only legitimate but healthy and good. The devil knows that the corruption of the best is the worst and that is the approach he consistently adopts and has certainly adopted here. Spiritual awakening absolutely demands the recognition of the corrupt agenda of the sexual revolution.

The modern liberal attitude has resulted from the attempt to replace real spirituality by appropriating some of its doctrines, which are dependent on recognition of their transcendent source for their truth, and interpreting them on a lower level so that the higher and more real level is obscured. It is a misrepresentation of spiritual truths by transferring them to the material world where their relevance is limited and must be seen in the light of the spiritual, which is always primary. Basically, it denies the vertical dimension of life and then takes values lost by that denial, and only true because of the reality of the vertical, and misapplies them to the horizontal. If you are serious about making spiritual progress, you must liberate yourself from its illusions, though without being driven to the opposite extreme, which will suit the demons just as well. However there will be no risk of that if you make God the focus of your thoughts, and love and wisdom the goals of your life.

What is the Left?

I am not interested in politics except as something seen in the light of spiritual truth. A proper understanding of metaphysics would render most political matters irrelevant in that the way to live would become obvious. But increasingly nowadays politics is used as a weapon against spiritual truth and that is why I must ask, what is the left? Is it merely a political point of view revolving around equality for all which believes in taking power from individuals and giving it to the State for the theoretical benefit of society as a whole, one that is espoused by the more intelligent amongst us as statistics appear to show, or is it, when you look beneath the surface, something rather different?

Let's get this idea that the more intelligent a person is, the more likely he or she is to adopt a leftish perspective out of the way first. This may be true up to a point, but that's largely because the training of the mind in the modern world is heavily slanted towards atheism and scientific materialism. That is the form of education we all receive, so the further we go in education as it is today, the more we will be indoctrinated by that mind-set. But those who are really able to think for themselves, which is surely a key factor in true intelligence, will see through the absurdity of materialism which, when properly analysed, is incoherent. It explains nothing and makes no sense, and can only be entertained seriously if vast elements of what life is and what a human being is are expunged from reality. If you're a materialist, you don't actually believe that you exist, not you as a real individual. Or anyone else for that matter, including those you love. Think about it.

Obviously the left is a political attitude outwardly but I believe its true origins lie in something deeper. I think that the real roots of what manifests in the world today as liberalism or the left (the two have become largely indistinguishable) is spiritual. Not spiritual as in deriving from God but spiritual as in coming from the so-called dark forces (interestingly sometimes described as those of the left hand path) which have set themselves up specifically against God and all that speaks of God, particularly the good, the beautiful and the true. I know that most people nowadays would ridicule such a notion but it has been understood in Christendom for as long as Christendom has existed and, if we dismiss it, our only grounds for doing so are that we dismiss the spiritual world entirely. I should stress that I am not proposing this duality of good and evil forces in a dualistic or Manichean sense. God is reality and there is nothing outside him. But there are fallen angels who, with their human accomplices, some deliberately so, most just a mixture of the spiritually ignorant and wrong thinking idealists, seek to corrupt and invert reality, and this world is their battleground.

Whether the ideology of the left was originally put through by forces favourable to God or by these demonic forces is not the point now. It is indisputable that in the 18th century new ideas did need to come through to bring about a greater measure of fairness in human society, but these were quickly co-opted and detached from any real spiritual framework which soon became secondary to the material side of things. From this we can deduce that, even if the movement was initially a heavenly inspiration, it was captured rather rapidly. It was directed towards things of this world to the more or less full exclusion of the next. Where there was a spiritual focus of some sort, it was a spirituality that stood in the shade of social or worldly issues and was considered in the light of those, which became primary.

Sometimes leftism, so called, is regarded as a Christian heresy. However, I see it as more like a perversion of Christianity, since heresies generally exaggerate certain aspects of truth while minimising or neglecting others but leftism completely eviscerates Christianity of the supernatural which is its whole point so it cannot be said to have any real relationship to Christianity at all. At best, you might say that it takes the horizontal part of Christianity while neglecting the vertical, transcendent part, but the horizontal without the vertical is unsupported and so falls to the ground.

But, however we define it, the spiritual intent of the left, or that of the true powers behind the left, is very clear today when we see it trying to remake reality according to its anti-God agenda. It does this through such things as erasing the natural differences between the sexes, cultural relativism, destroying or inverting the hierarchy of truth, goodness and beauty, and placing excessive emphasis on reason as the best guide to life thereby tarring faith and intuition with the brush of superstition. And when we observe it trying to dismantle traditional institutions which have evolved with a spiritual purpose (for instance, marriage) both by attacking them externally and by trying to corrupt them from within, we have another pointer to the true agenda of those behind it. Many of those involved in all this are not aware of its true purpose but consider themselves to be acting in the name of progress. In some respects, they might be doing so which makes the picture more complicated for those who only see the appearance of things. But look beneath the surface and a different picture takes shape. Then you see that the establishment of secondary truths is being used as an excuse to destroy primary ones, and even these secondary truths are soon discarded when they've served their purpose.

A lot of what the main drivers of the cultural and academic left believe and assert comes from their fear and hatred of God. This goes back at least as far as Rousseau, the French Revolution and Marx. They want to unmake reality and remake it according to their materialistic and atheistic theories so that God has no place in it. This is one reason they attack that fundamental truth of the two sexes so relentlessly. If they can destroy something so basic and so universally acknowledged as that, they have gone a long way towards driving the truth of God from the universe. Or so they hope. They can never fully succeed because eventually the false society they are creating will collapse, either from external attack or internal despair but they can do great damage to the state of people's souls before that happens, and that is the principal purpose of their unseen masters, whether they are aware of this or not.

With the two sexes they have used the excuse that the similarities are more important than the differences to deny the fact of the differences and that these are intrinsic and essential. And this is a large part of the problem. The left is frequently dishonest and uses lies to advance its distortion of truth or else, more subtly, it uses lesser truths to force out greater ones. At one time, I thought that people on the left were mistaken but honest, and no doubt many are, but it's increasingly obvious that the main drivers of the revolution have always been people of bad faith in that their motivations are not what is claimed. The real origin of their position can frequently be seen as resentment of others and hatred of the good. That is why they are so adversarial and disputatious. Of course, the foot soldiers are not always like this but they are spiritually blind, and they often have something of their leaders' faults in them, too. I am not here saying anything as crude and simplistic as left bad, right good, for all of us are sinners in our different ways. Nonetheless the fact is that the denial of God and of the true good is at the roots of left wing ideology, acknowledged or not, while the right in its proper form (qualifying adjective stressed) is essentially religious, of which more in a moment.

I have maintained that mainstream leftism is atheistic, if not actively anti-theistic, and so it is. But many people nowadays who have a vague and unformed sort of spirituality also embrace a liberal perspective, so why, one must ask, is so much modern, as opposed to traditional, spirituality left leaning? The short answer to this is that it is human and this world centred. It does not look to God the Creator as the *summum bonum* of life. Nor does it acknowledge the fact that we are fallen and in need of redemption. It sees human beings as they are now as basically good and perfectible if only they are treated nicely. There's no need to repent because you, as you are now, are already good and it just needs to come out. Perhaps I exaggerate to make a point but I see left-leaning spirituality as essentially interested in spirituality for its fruits and the feelings you might get from it, not from love of God or the sanctification of the soul. Generally speaking, the modern left has little use for God, who it tends to cast in the light of an oppressor which, no doubt, from the point of view of a self-willed rebel against truth, he is.

Nothing here should be taken as implying that current versions of the right have any kind of handle on goodness and truth. No approach to life without a proper spiritual understanding at its heart can ever be right. I've criticised the left because of its anti-Christian agenda which is plain to see. It either seeks to destroy Christianity from outside or deform it from within, and it's been very successful in both those tactics. The right has not been used to the same extent, but a secular right, given power, could be as materialistic as the left, albeit in a different way. I can also envisage a scenario in which a version of the right could be used to advance an authoritarian form of religion which effectively rejects love and imposes rigid control with no room for dissension. But, speaking in cultural rather than economic terms, that is not what we have in the West in the 21st century. Nonetheless, while the left has distorted love by separating it from its origins in God, flattening it out, "egalitarianising" it and then reducing it to the horizontal plane only, so the right could potentially similarly distort the idea of truth. Both, of course, can only corrupt realities because there is nothing else other than these realities, just as evil can only mar – it cannot make.

Setting any future possible scenarios aside, it could be objected that most people on the right nowadays have no more interest in God than those on the left. This is true but it's because they are only on the right in certain matters, for example, economic. In most other particulars, they have absorbed and copied the current liberal ethos. The fact is that all true right wing thought recognises a higher reality and a higher authority than the secular, materialistic world of the left. So what really distinguishes the two sides is the acknowledgement of God and the acceptance that we are here in this world for a spiritual purpose. I realise this is not the usual definition but I think you will find that, if you strip both back to their roots, this is what you will discover.

Thus, although the left claims to be seeking a more just and humane society, the fact that it does so without reference to the Creator, and according to the scientific/materialistic vision means that, for all its claims to improve the lot of man in this world, it immeasurably diminishes his true status by separating him from his spiritual source and being. Its focus on the collective strips him of freedom and real individuality, denying him the chance to grow as he should, but above all its rejection of spiritual reality cuts him off from light and life in their real forms. Consequently the most you can say about the left is that it devotes itself to making the world perfect for acorns, ignoring the fact that acorns are meant to grow into oaks. It is therefore the ideology of stunted spiritual growth.

Jesus said he did not come to abolish the Law and the Prophets but to fulfil them. He also said that whoever relaxed the least of the commandments of the Law, and taught others to do the same, would be called the least in the Kingdom of Heaven. What does this tell us? It means that the preservation of the Law and the Prophets is essential. You can, you should, build on them but they are the foundation. It is true that what does not grow will die but it must grow from its roots. Jesus was progressive in a certain sense but his progressiveness was completely grounded in an innate conservatism. Modern progressives, in contrast, seek to build a future on the shattered ruins of the past, the destruction of the Law and the Prophets. They do not have divine sanction.

Everything requires balance, and you might think it is only the excesses of the left I have been talking about here. The truth is, though, that the excesses were built into it from the start. They were, if not inevitable, highly probable. It did not take much time to go from seeking a degree of social justice in this world, to being more concerned with that than one's spiritual state, to the rejection of God, to the overturning of the natural order of being. Thus, while liberal ideas may have been of use at one time, to act as a corrective and counterweight to past corruption of ideas about the nature of God and hierarchy, they should never have been taken as a basic philosophy of life in themselves. The best you can say about the left is that it is like a strong medicine which is useful when the patient is sick but does not form part of a healthy diet. If it becomes one's main nourishment it may turn into the poison of atheistic materialism as it has today.

The essential point I am trying to make here is that, starting in the 19th century then increasingly throughout the 20th, and especially since the end of World War Two, the left has been used by demonic forces to unmake Man. I am not referring to the economic side of things which, spiritually speaking, is not particularly important, but to the cultural side. It is this that is used as a weapon against God. Of course, the left has achieved some good things but that is hardly the point when its overall effect has been to separate Man from his Maker.

When this piece first appeared in an earlier form, I was asked a question which I think is worth including here as a postscript.

Q. I used to be involved with various New Age groups but found that every single one of them assumed the truth of liberalism, and if you expressed any other opinion they looked almost shocked. Your opinion was branded as "Piscean" meaning old-fashioned, prejudiced and ignorant rather than "Aquarian" or liberal and enlightened in social and cultural matters, and the strong implication was you couldn't possibly be spiritual. What do you think is going on here?

It's true that most non-traditional forms of spirituality are politically and culturally liberal. It wasn't always so but now it's just an assumption that this is what a good person should be. I actually believe it is one of the tests of the present time. Are you able to think for yourself as to what goodness and truth really are or do you follow the fashionable crowd of perceived goodness and truth, assuming you're in the vanguard of progress?

Probably that has come about for several reasons. First of all, most of the intelligentsia is like this. Liberalism is seen as the default intelligent person's position now, but it has largely come from non-spiritual if not anti-spiritual sources so should be treated with suspicion on that account alone. It is not a response to any traditional spiritual teaching but a manifestation of the democratic spirit and therefore a political thing. But because most people today are educated in liberalism before they encounter serious spirituality, they bring their preconceived notions with them, and their spirituality has to fit in to their already existing liberal world view.

Then there's love. Everyone knows you should love, and liberalism is perceived as being more in line with that doctrine because it tends to treat everybody the same. It is more "loving". But love is not indiscriminate nor does it deny truth, and, though we were told by Jesus to be as innocent as doves, we were also told to be as wise as serpents. Love should not be used as an excuse to deny spiritual reality, which is hierarchical when in expression, nor should it be limited to man as he is in this world. What appears to be love to the outer man might not be at all when considered in the light of the whole man. Obviously, love is good but real love can only be understood in the context of the whole picture, and liberalism denies most of the picture as it is an ideology focused on men and women as they are in this world. It doesn't think in terms of the next.

Then there's sex. Traditional spirituality understood that

this incredibly powerful force must be contained or it will be destructive rather than creative. Unless it is contained (in marriage) and if it is seen as an end in itself, it will lead an individual or a society away from any true spiritual development or self-transcendence to a concern with self-fulfilment; that is, a fulfilment of the lower, earthly self rather than the soul or spiritual self. An over-concern with sex leads to spiritual desensitivity precisely because it is a form of spiritual energy translated to the physical plane. So if you give free rein to this energy in a physical sense, you are unable to express it spiritually. But for liberals, everyone should have the freedom to do as they wish if they don't harm another, and sexual freedom has become one of their most important freedoms. What they don't see is that, in the context of spiritual truth, you harm yourself when you pursue certain apparent freedoms – as you also do society as a whole. Controlling sex is often seen as a vice or a weakness rather than a virtue by the liberal mind, but that is because many people don't want to control it and look for an excuse not to do so.

Then there is freedom itself. For the liberal, freedom, like love, is seen as a universal good but in fact, like love, it must be seen in the context of, and be subordinate to, the reality of God. Taken out of its proper context, as it is in liberalism, it becomes a means to extend the dominion of the unrepentant, autonomous self. The restraint of sex and freedom, so important in traditional monastic disciplines that were founded on chastity and obedience, has been rejected by liberal spirituality, but why have these been rejected? If you look beneath the surface, you will see it's because liberal spirituality wants to extend rather than transcend the boundaries of the natural self.

Following on from all these things, we can see that modern, non-traditional spirituality is human-centred. That means that implicitly, if not explicitly, personal growth or healing rather than salvation or sanctification is the order of the day. For most New Age type spirituality, humanity is not regarded as fallen and in need of repentance but full of spiritual potential which just needs to come out if you use the right techniques. No doubt we do have great potential, Jesus told us we did, but this will only come out after there is true repentance which is an admission that you of yourself are nothing and everything derives from God. Indeed, as my teachers told me, **"The Master Jesus and all the Masters of old knew they were as nothing and all they were came from the Creator".** Any form of spirituality which does not have this front and centre is false or, if that sounds too harsh to you, it is shallow and will really not amount to much.

And here we come to the heart of the matter. God is not an important figure for the New Age. He is either surplus to requirements or a patriarchal embarrassment or something to be gone beyond or so transformed by having to adapt to human interests that he is not God at all any longer. But God the Father, God the Creator of Heaven and Earth, God as Person, is not important. If he were then everything else would have to fit into that, as it should, but when he is dismissed or downgraded or changed into something else then spirituality is not about man making himself right with God but about man, in effect, becoming God himself. And here I think we come to the real reason that New Age spirituality is liberal. It is because the true motive of the New Age is to supplant God with man; that is, the human being becomes divine of itself and without reference to its Creator.

Some liberal and spiritual people would say they do believe in God, but actually what they often seem to mean by this is a sort of idealised mother figure who loves all her children as they are now, and doesn't require them to change or grow in any serious way. Someone who comes down to them where they are now, rather than someone who requires them to go up. Someone who offers rebirth without prior death. This is not the real God as taught by all serious religions, especially Christianity, who is love and truth together not just unconditional, undiscriminating love. Nor, may I say, was it how the Masters who spoke to me were. They had greater love than any human being I have ever come across but they expressed this in the context of the knowledge that we on this Earth are out of kilter with truth and need to put ourselves right. We need to straighten up and straighten out. Of course, God loves us but he loves the real us, created by him in his image, not the false self we have created for ourselves in our own image down here.

Looking at this another way, you could say that those who think of themselves as spiritual and liberal focus largely on God immanent to the exclusion of God transcendent, but the former must always be seen in the light of the latter. For us, God is transcendent before he is immanent.

As for the Piscean and Aquarian jibe, don't worry about that. Outer things may change but inner realities don't nor does the path to God. Yes, it may grow and develop and take in more of truth but any higher understanding of truth must build on the old, not replace it with something quite new and different. This is how things work in the spiritual world and it is how they work in nature too. Besides, you could counter that traditionally Aquarius is ruled by Saturn, regarded as a malefic planet, so it may not indicate quite such a brave new world as normally painted by New Age enthusiasts.

Essentially what I am saying here is that those who see themselves as liberal and spiritual don't understand the spiritual because they view it in the context of themselves and this world, rather than in that of God, which is the only true way.

I would also say that if you are liberal and spiritual, one of those two elements is eventually going to have to override the other. Is it the reality of this world or the next that is more important to you?

Awakening from Delusion

In his second epistle to the Thessalonians, St Paul writes of a "strong delusion" that God will send to those who refuse to love truth. This seems a bit unfair. Why make things more difficult for those who are already erring? But it echoes Jesus's statement that more will be given to those who already have, while those who do not have will lose even what little they do have.

What's going on here? I think Jesus is saying that the act of opening one's heart to God allows you to receive all kinds of spiritual benefits, while closing your heart to God will cut you off from the spiritual world so you plunge further and further into darkness and delusion. Note that spiritual benefits does not mean the good things of life. It may entail suffering and hardship but you will be brought closer to truth and eventual release from the chains of this world. You will be led to liberation from sin and darkness, and release into eternal life.

What St Paul says is something similar. Those who deny God are given what they want. Which is a lie. Their initial act is a rejection of the truth that is both within them and also proclaimed in both nature and scripture if we look with unprejudiced eyes. This rejection is often caused by egotism in that it is an act of will not intellect. They have chosen untruth so God sends them more of that, not to punish them but to give them the results of their decision. Obviously, God does not punish in a mean, vengeful sense, but acts and choices have consequences and the strong delusion is the consequence of the denial of truth. You might say that God gives you enough rope to hang yourself with if that's what you want to do. You have a test of your spiritual integrity and if you are not equal to that, then the strong delusion is provided for you to confirm you in your ignorance. Your heart could not be tested if there was not a plausible alternative to belief in God. The strong delusion is an apparently viable alternative that can be used to justify unbelief if that's what you want to do, even if, when examined with honesty and clarity, it does not hold up.

So, what is this strong delusion? Assuming we are living in the end times, what could it be? Incidentally, it is widely accepted by many serious spiritual thinkers that we are indeed living in something approximating to the end times or latter days. For however far man has fallen in the past, he has always known that he has fallen, whereas now he likes to think he is progressing, so much has he lost sight of his origins and destiny. It is only recently that he has sunk so low from a spiritual perspective that he believes himself to be higher than ever.

Assuming, then, that these are the end times, what is the delusion? There are several candidates, ranging from materialism to atheistic Marxism to Darwinian evolution, which sees intelligent conscious life as arising from inert matter through random mutation of its component parts and the survival of the fittest, to science and positivism in general. It could be any of these but today there is actually something that combines them all, and that is what is called leftism, the popular belief system of the modern world.

The strong delusion must be shared by many, if not most, people. It must be the accepted wisdom of the worldly elite. It must be anti-Christian in spirit. It must corrupt nature. And it must be thought of as good in the light of how we see the world. All these things apply to leftism in its modern version. Leftism is the strong delusion of the modern world.

Which brings us to the title of this chapter. As far as the present day is concerned, awakening from delusion means awakening to the truth that modern left/liberal thought with its grounding in rational humanism is a false doctrine. That certainly doesn't mean abandoning the humanitarianism that is the justification of the leftist claim to truth, but seeing that in the light of the supreme reality of God not of man.

For the religion of man, which is what leftism amounts to, is a false religion that redefines what is good by treating the material as an end in itself instead of perceiving it as an expression of the spiritual.

To take just one example, pertinent at the moment, leftism sees it as the right thing to do to help a man who wants to become a woman do so because a person has the right to be what he or she wants to be. But the spiritual view sees this as a rebellion against God's will for you and a refusal to live your life as intended. In terms of Hinduism, it is rejecting your karma (destined path) and your dharma (duty in life). And, as it is said, it's better to do your own dharma badly than somebody else's well.

Furthermore, to fight nature is to fight God who made nature. Nature is meant to be transformed by grace not reconfigured by man. Quite obviously this doesn't mean such people should not be treated with compassion, but should real compassion seek to cure a spiritual malaise by material means? Or should it direct an individual towards resolution at a higher level?

So, we must awaken from the false idea that man is meant for man and see men and women as meant for God, which means see them in the light of the reality of God, not the false reality of their own light. Awakening from delusion means acknowledging the reality of the vertical axis which we have completely lost contact with, seeing everything as only existing on a horizontal plane. It means acknowledging transcendence. For when we come right down to it, the strong delusion is the denial of transcendence.

Now, clearly I don't mean rejecting leftism is all that is required for full spiritual awakening. The main thing will always be the acknowledgement of the reality of God and living in the light of that reality. But those who believe they have awoken to the truth of God and the soul will still be half asleep until they also see through the "strong delusion" that is leftism, for leftism is the attempt to remake the world without reference to God. This is a large part of the test of the present day.

What we can take from this is that any theoretical spiritual awakening which does not reject the leftist restructuring of the world, including the sexual revolution, is at best a partial awakening. It may even be a false awakening since the fact that something is called spiritual does not necessarily make it true. There are many forms of spirituality that are still rooted in illusion because they come from the lower mind.

For bear in mind that if you adopt a spiritual position and fit that into your pre-existing worldly assumptions, you are seeing the higher in terms of the lower. Proper spiritual awakening demands that one reassess *all* one's previous ideas and see them as from above. If your spirituality is cut down to accord with already existing beliefs, it is more or less useless. That is because the point of spiritual awakening is to orientate us towards the soul, the spiritual component of our being. If this soul is seen through the lens of the worldly self then it is not seen at all. The soul is not an extension of the earthly being but the true spiritual self that exists beyond that, and which is our connection to God. The fallen earthly self can never be spiritual in and of itself, and any spirituality emanating from or conforming to it is a false spirituality which is still part of the delusion.

Truth and Love

The gateway to the kingdom of heaven has two pillars which are truth and love, and you must conform yourself to both of these to a high degree before you are worthy to enter. That's a tall order as no one can be perfect, perfection coming only through the grace of God. But you must attune yourself to both these two qualities as best you can, holding them in a more or less equal balance in your mind and heart.

This balance is important for without it you will not only be unbalanced (obviously) but even lose touch with that which you are over-emphasising. That is because each suggests and assumes the other, and if one is over-privileged at the expense of the other it means that you are not responding to reality as a whole and in its totality but to a personal interpretation of reality. With true love always goes wisdom. With proper wisdom, there is always love. If you follow one of these paths and neglect the other then you are surely following a false path for you are not even following the reality of your chosen path, merely your idea about it.

The devil exploits our sense of fairness and will to do good to the detriment of truth so that truth ends up being denied. You might say that if love is observed, what does truth matter? That's just foolish sentimentality. Love is not all you need by any means. If you do not honour truth above all, and seek to incline your being to it, you will have no chance of aligning yourself with the reality of God. You will remain enclosed in the worldly mind and that means you won't even be observing love. All you will have will be an idea about love. And so it is, by pushing us too much towards a false image of love, the devil effectively cuts us off from truth.

Same sex marriage is a case in point. Any clear-thinking person, heterosexual or homosexual, can see that it is a contradiction in terms, a metaphysical impossibility like a square circle, but we have been deceived into accepting it because we wish to be just, and because we think that the short term happiness of individuals in this world matters more than their education for eternity. That is, of course, because we do not acknowledge eternity or, if we think we do, it's only an eternity that is seen in the light of the desires, aims and purposes of this world. We are putting the earthly personality ahead of the spiritual soul and either denying the latter or else seeing it as an extension of the former. None of this will get us anywhere except deeper into illusion and spiritual ignorance.

But the devil can also exploit the idea of truth to get us to deny love. The Spanish Inquisition is a typical example from history, but many cultures have damned and ostracised those who don't conform to their ideals. The protection of truth is important. There are so many arrows aimed at its heart, so many attempts to corrupt and distort it, so many half-truths masquerading as the full version, that we all have a responsibility to fight for truth. But we should not let this fight lead us into blaspheming against love, just as we should not take the reality of love, as a spiritual truth, for a reason to offer love to everything equally, regardless of its approximation to truth. Things that contradict truth should not be loved in their expression even if, in their essence, they are due love. The classic example of this is in the Christian exhortation to hate the sin but love the sinner. In fact, this saying cuts right across the divide between love and truth, successfully reconciling them both.

We live at a time of increasing polarisation when worldly extremes confront each other in mutual incomprehension and antagonism. These can only be reconciled from a spiritual perspective which transcends both of them, and I mean a real spiritual perspective not a spurious one that derives from either of these worldly viewpoints. One of them is a distortion on a lower plane of love and one of them is a distortion on a lower plane of truth. Neither has much relation to real love or truth but, just as evil has no reality in itself but can only exist as a perversion of the real, so the worldly viewpoints which dominate today can only arise from a spiritual reality, albeit one misconceived, distorted and at many removes.

If we see truth and love, like justice and mercy, as the Father and Mother of reality it becomes obvious that we need both for a proper understanding of life. Either one without the other leads to imbalance. The roots of modern political division are to be found in this imbalance, though the focus of the devil's attempt to corrupt humanity in recent times has been through the exploitation of a false idea of love without truth, of oneness without discernment, you might also say. Perhaps he will try the other approach at some time in the future, but he cannot deceive us if we stay centred in the reality of God.

The Pharisees condemned Christ because he favoured mercy over the law, in their eyes, anyway. Actually, he did not. He just didn't reduce mercy to insignificance when set against the law. He kept the balance between the two and responded to each situation on an individual basis rather than an inflexible, set in stone one. Unlike the Pharisees, slaves to ideology, he treated human beings in a human way, not as impersonal objects to be fitted into an unbending dogma. But he also worked from law and truth, as can be evidenced in numerous passages of the Gospels, for example when he said that he did not come to abolish the Law but to fulfil it or when, in John chapter 14 verse 15, he stated clearly and unambiguously, "If you love me, keep my commandments."

The point is Jesus looked into the heart and if he saw goodness there he aimed to bring it out. He saw rigidity in the hearts of the Pharisees so contested them. He did not do this because of their adherence to the Law but because of their hard-heartedness in enforcing it. He looked into the heart of sinners and sometimes he saw true spiritual feeling there, albeit overlaid by sin. So he encouraged them to come to him, but that required a willingness on their part to repent of their sins, certainly to recognise that they were in a state of sin and do their best to move out of that. He reached out to people and called them to repent and change. If they were not willing to do that, and wanted spiritual reward without being willing to renounce their sinful ways, he would not have persevered with them. They would have been as bad as the Pharisees, albeit at the other end of the spectrum of sinfulness. Their spiritual sincerity and desire to change were paramount.

It can never be repeated too often. Jesus did not come to make us happy in our earthly lives but to bring us to holiness. He loved and he forgave, but above all he was the Truth, and he required all those who followed him to walk in the way of truth. If they did not, well then, they could not be his disciples. You cannot have Jesus and sin any more than you can have God and Mammon. If you love me, keep my commandments means if you don't keep, or at least try to keep, my commandments then you don't love me. Jesus brought mercy but not a cheap and false mercy that overlooked sin, because sin is fundamentally what separates a person from God. To warn people against sin and the spiritual self-injury that results from it is not hard-hearted but truly merciful because it frees the soul from captivity.

We are all sinners but the spiritual person recognises this, accepts it and tries to put it right. He doesn't try to excuse or justify his sin or deny that it is one. Likewise, the spiritual teacher will talk of God's forgiveness but forgiveness is conditional on proper repentance. Again, truth and love must go together. You cannot have one without the other.

Spiritual awakening, if it is to be genuine and sustainable, requires awakening to the understanding that truth and love lie at the heart of the universe. I believe it is through the imagination that we can start to realise this, for imagination is the key that unlocks the door to the higher worlds. It is the forerunner of intuition or spiritual intelligence, and I have always felt that those who deny the reality of God lack imagination. Such people might think they have imagination, and be affronted if it is implied they don't, but what they call their imagination is earthbound in that, though it might extend horizontally as far as the (mind's) eye may see, it cannot rise much above ground level. It is a flat thing that is not proper imagination at all for it cannot see behind outer things to their inner essence, which is what real imagination is all about. Unsupported reason, which works by proceeding from one thing to another, can never see the spiritual reality of truth and love, but imagination, which perceives directly, can. Start cultivating the eye of inner vision now but remember when you do that imagination still needs to develop into proper intuition, and that can only happen when you begin to align your inner being with the reality behind truth and love instead of responding to these from the outside.

Feminism and Love

While we are on the subject of political responses to spiritual problems, doomed to failure by their very nature, and quite likely to make matters worse, we should consider the case of feminism. But first let us remind ourselves that while the doctrines of liberalism, of which feminism is a branch, may seem reasonable according to its own lights, its view of how the world is structured is false. How can you correctly respond to reality when you fundamentally misconceive what reality is? Everything boils down to metaphysics, meaning how you perceive reality to be. If you perceive it incorrectly, for example through the distorting lens of atheistic materialism, then your opinions about the world, and how it is or should be, will be wrong. If you are operating from faulty information, you will almost certainly come to a faulty conclusion.

Anyone who sees feminism as one of the typical errors of the modern age often finds it necessary to keep his own counsel these days. What is the point of getting into an argument over this dogma of the educated elite, this prejudice now so installed in people's minds that they are unable to reflect objectively about it?

But the feminist error is so damaging to human beings and their relationships with each other that here I would like to look at why it is an error and how, far from being a touchstone of enlightenment, it actually alienates us from our true selves and from God. Evidently to say such a thing in polite company nowadays is sufficient to be shown the door, yet I persist in thinking that deep down many people suspect the truth about this but cover it up for various reasons to do with power, personal advantage, a misconceived sense of justice or simply seeking to fit in.

Let's get something out of the way first of all. There was

originally a need for some kind of readjustment between the sexes. The balance certainly had tipped too far on to the masculine side. But to go from that to what we have now, where the essential difference between the sexes is dismissed as cultural, and the feminine apes the masculine to grab a share of male power, is altogether another matter.

The starting point of any discussion of this topic should be the statement in Genesis, "Male and female created he them". I say that is the starting point, not in the sense that Biblical authority cannot be questioned but because, as statements go, it contains so much in so little. Unpack it and it points to the truth that the sexes are different, complementary, and, because not the same, not equal. All that is contained inside those six words. And the order in which the two sexes are mentioned is also important. They are two halves of a whole but one comes before the other in the context of their creation, even though both are of equal worth. Now, I submit that everybody knows this. It has been the universal human belief across all cultures and all times until the last couple of hundred years, which coincides, not coincidentally, with the rise of materialism and atheism. It is one of the few beliefs that pretty much all humans have ever shared. What arrogance to think that we have discovered something that nobody else could see! To say that women have been suppressed for all that time and in all those places, and have only recently been able to shake off that suppression rather implies a stupidity and ineffectiveness on the part of the female sex which would be a counter-productive argument for feminists to make. It's more logical to think that everyone simply recognised a natural state of affairs that wasn't always perfectly expressed but, on balance, was seen as correct. Of course, there has been injustice at times. No one would dispute that, but that is the result of the abuse of male power. It is no reason to conclude that the traditional basis of the male/female relationship is wrong.

I want to approach this matter by asking what are the qualities that the ideal male should demonstrate and what are those of the ideal female. I think that if we understand these then we should have a better idea of what men and women are and what they ought to be to each other. Those schooled in the ways of relativism and materialism might reject this notion of ideals or archetypes, and assert that anyone can be what they want to be, but all I can really say to them is that they are wrong. They don't have, or won't acknowledge, the full facts. And they are not only rejecting spiritual truth. They are rejecting nature, too. In fact, they are rejecting everything except ideological theory, very possibly based on wishful thinking, and they need to address what it is in them that is making them do that. It is not reason and it's not intuition, so it must be something else.

I have come up with three main qualities for each sex. These are not meant as definitive qualities above all others. You could undoubtedly come up with different ones which would be equally valid. But they are, I consider, fairly fundamental and they do capture something of the archetype of male and female. And it is the archetype of our sex that each one of us should be attempting to manifest, expressed through the unique form of our own individuality. We are most ourselves when we do this. We all have a pattern to which we should be true and to which we should be attempting to conform. Only when we do this will we achieve real fulfilment and the sense of being what we should be. The pattern of our sex is only one such but it is a very important one. Inevitably, in this fallen world which has long gone astray, there are always going to be exceptions, but these exceptions have to be seen in the light of the rule and cannot be given equal authenticity. They must be known as exceptions and treated accordingly, with compassion and fairness but not with equal significance, or the whole balance and order of nature will be disturbed. And when the balance of nature is disturbed and the order of creation disordered, there will be a reaction and it won't be a happy one.

The pre-eminent male qualities are nobility, authority and courage. Men should conform to these. The female equivalents are beauty, purity and gentleness, and women should incarnate these. This tells us that leadership is largely male and the compassion that balances and humanises that leadership is largely female. Not a popular thought today but nonetheless one that corresponds to archetypal reality. However, at the same time, each sex should include the qualities of the other, though expressed within the context of their own nature, which is primary and determining. Thus, a woman's intellect manifests in the context of her femininity, and a man's emotions should work within the context of his masculinity. Similarly for will and love, which will be expressed differently in each case. I repeat that all human beings have to develop the full panoply of human qualities but each sex should express these within the reality of their maleness or femaleness. If that is not the case then there is an imbalance and that leads to disorder. This is an ideal and the human race is a long way from living according to any ideal, but we should at least recognise and aspire towards it as the template for what we should be. The nearer we get to it, the better we will be. And vice versa.

There are those who claim that the erosion of difference we are witnessing today points towards a kind of divine androgyny of the future, and so is progressive in evolutionary terms. This ignores two important facts. One, in the beginning God created humanity as man and woman, and this duality reproduces that of spirit and matter, subject and object, life and form, which lies at the heart of creation and without which there could be nothing. And two, just as Jesus came to fulfil the law not abolish it, so life proceeds in an organic, evolutionary manner, building on what came before not eradicating it and starting anew. Violent revolution is contrary to the divine method. Grace perfects nature. It doesn't reject it. Duality is central to manifestation, and so are man and woman who are the two poles of existence and the expression of the purpose of creation, which was relationship. In other words, love.

The war between the sexes, in which feminism represents a major battle, came about as a result of the Fall. Unfortunately, the idea of the Fall, a rift between Creator and created brought about by the misuse of self-will, is not recognised in today's secular world and so the symptoms of it are not acknowledged either. This is why feminism is seen as a good instead of the error it actually is. Why an error? Because it is essentially a war against femininity and an attempt to unbalance creation. That is what is behind it. Feminism makes women abandon their femininity and become imitators of masculinity, and so the civilising, softening, spiritually receptive, wise, nurturing aspects of true womanhood are lost. It is often egotism and desire for power disguised as a search for equality. And that tells us why many women support it, even though it denies the deepest part of their nature which is left to atrophy. Or perhaps that is only true of the feminist leaders and many women are actually victims of it, going along with it because the world tells them to and because of its supposedly egalitarian aspect, egalitarianism being regarded as the basic truth of the modern world even though a child should be able to see it as a completely false doctrine. The child would see through it because of natural instinct but an intellectual fails to see it because he is too tied up in theory. A wise man, though, sees it because he perceives that life is not just one thing, unity, but two things, unity and plurality, a ladder with steps, and in the context of the latter there is always a hierarchy. Nowhere in the entire universe is there equality. God does not do equality.

But why do so many men support it? From my experience, the reasons range from a desire to seem fair and just, to going along with the status quo, to gain sexual advantage, reluctance to accept masculine responsibility or even loss of confidence and resentment at more successful or powerful males. And, of course, there are also many who logically must support it because of their materialism and atheism of which feminism is a product. And there are, too, those whose understanding of past injustices towards the female sex leads them into the opposite error. So, a mixture of good and bad motives but all still lacking in wisdom or insight.

St Paul says that the man should be the head of the family. This is in line with the perception that natural authority is a masculine attribute, a deeply unfashionable view nowadays, to say the least. But what if we extended this to say that woman should be the heart of the family? Would it seem so unjust then? The head should rule the heart but it should also allow itself to be guided by the heart when appropriate. That way lies harmony. Of course, a man has a heart and a woman has a head but each sex should still conform to its prototype if the natural and spiritual order is to be maintained. When what should be the heart tries to become the head, as now, what becomes of the real heart? Spiritual chaos ensues as it most certainly has done in our prideful and foolish times.

There is a lot more to say on this subject but I'd like to conclude this chapter by pointing out that when the differences between men and women are eroded, as they are now, the relationship between them becomes much more a matter of crude sexual attraction on the one hand and competition on the other, and the possibility of real love, which depends on being fulfilled by the complementary other, much harder. That is why I have titled this chapter feminism and love, for feminism destroys love between the sexes just as surely as any aggressively male culture in which women are treated as inferiors does. It is, in fact, very close to being a mirror image of that.

So feminism is fundamentally an anti-love ideology. Insofar as it drives women to usurp the masculine, it is destructive of a proper complementary relationship between the sexes. It can be perceived as a product of the rebelliousness of spiritual adolescence and a sign of the end times, when values are inverted.

You could say it is Eve once again succumbing to temptation and having another bite of the apple in the attempt to become a god. You might even say it is misogynistic because it rejects and devalues what women really are and what they uniquely have to offer in the attempt to make them more masculine.

The reader might regard this as a rather one-sided appraisal and say that everything has the defects of its qualities, and I have concentrated on the dark side of feminism here, ignoring its positive aspects. To which I would reply that, setting aside you could say this about almost anything, you have to see where something leads before pronouncing it as on the whole good or bad. Obviously there have been some benefits that have come from feminism. If not it would have been doomed from the start, but on the whole what are its effects? And what is the real aim behind it? And I would say that its effects are largely destructive on an individual level, a cultural level and especially on a spiritual level. By reducing archetypes to stereotypes it limits men and women to purely material beings, cutting them off from their higher nature which, if approached at all, is approached from the false position of a material being trying to bend the spiritual to its own pseudo-reality instead of conforming itself to the reality of the spiritual. As for the real aim behind it, it is clear when looked at with the eye of spiritual vision that this is the separation of man (as in the human being) from his spiritual nature, hence from God. It is the materialisation of man through the deformation of the human archetype, the destruction of the family and the fermenting of competition and conflict between the sexes. When all is said and done, it is not inspired by love but by rebellion, and its results are the fruits of that.

Well, I am quite aware that many people in today's world will completely reject what I have written here and interpret it as the prejudices of a bigoted male. That is a pity. But my belief is that modern feminism disrespects true spiritual womanhood almost as much as male arrogance. Perhaps the devil is afraid of the spiritual influence of women when orientated toward the Good, and that is why he has sought to undermine it through feminism, which you can see as a materialistic attack on the imagination that effectively cuts a woman off from the deeper mysteries of her own being, to the loss of both women and men. Here's a radical thought for your consideration. In the West for nearly 2,000 years the ideal woman has been Mary, the Mother of God. Is this an outmoded concept or does it remain eternally true?

Dark Powers

Several times throughout these pages I have alluded to demonic forces that seek to derail the spiritual unfoldment of humanity. This is an idea that has always been acknowledged by religion but would be rejected by most people nowadays as superstitious nonsense. We are too sophisticated to believe such childish fairy tales. But once again, it is a matter of metaphysics and appreciating the nature of reality. When we know that there are spirits who have fallen so far that they have, in full awareness, denied their Creator, and who now seek to undermine the creation because of a perverted will, one lost in hatred and resentment of the Good, then much that occurs in the world becomes easier to understand. These beings with their agenda of spiritual corruption have been behind a great deal of what has occurred in the 20th and 21st centuries. Certainly, they have been active and present for as long as humanity has been on this earth but they have been especially influential over the last century or so. Possibly this is because we are reaching some kind of crisis point in the spiritual development of humanity.

If we assume that human evolutionary unfoldment proceeds from its early, passive state of absorption in nature (unconscious union) on to our current mode of self-consciousness in which individual will and intelligence are developed (conscious separation) and then on again to an eventual Christ-like state of active and full participation in the whole of life (conscious union) going from instinct to intellect (or reason) to intuition as primary modes of cognition in the process, then we can see that the time of greatest separation from the spiritual source is the time when we would be most vulnerable to demonic attack. That time is now and this explains why attempts to first subvert and then invert truth have been so intensive in recent decades. Think of the evolutionary path as an arc, something like a U. We are currently right at the bottom of that arc, furthest in consciousness from the sense of God and therefore most susceptible to the influence to unmake us and remake us not in the image of God but in the image of something else.

My teachers told me that the greater progress a soul makes, the more it is assailed by evil forces. They thought this worth saying many times. Traditional stories of saints and martyrs have often included incidents of demonic assault. Consider poor St Anthony, attacked on a regular basis, or St Dunstan who eventually got so fed up that he seized the devil who was tormenting him with a pair of tongs. We might think of these stories as either allegorical or else the product of mental disturbance, but it is perfectly possible that these highly spiritual souls were able to perceive beings on non-material planes. And, even if we don't take the stories literally, we should still be aware that all souls on the path are attacked by dark forces who attempt to lead them astray. This they do by searching out their weaknesses, anger, pride and all the rest, and influencing their thoughts in a negative direction. You may not accept this but I can tell you that any knowledgeable spiritual teacher would confirm it. This is not merely a personification of psychological responses in a person's own mind. It is real.

In just the same way as individuals on the path are attacked, so is humanity. Unfortunately, humanity in general, being less spiritually mature than those among it who are sincerely seeking God, is all too easy to corrupt. Resistance to this is not a question of intelligence. Indeed, if intelligence goes with pride, which it often does, it may succumb more easily. Rather, it is a question of spiritual integrity and discrimination which members of the modern elite are not always amongst the first to possess. Christ's words that it is harder for a rich man to get to heaven than for a camel to go through the eye of a needle do not just apply to those who are materially wealthy. They can also apply to those endowed with mental riches, especially if these are divorced from humility.

The devil (which term I use not to refer to an individual but the dark forces in general) has fought his battle over the last couple of centuries on two main fronts. Firstly, he has encouraged materialism and atheism, often in seemingly innocuous or even apparently progressive ways, such as through the discoveries of science. I do not say science itself is bad but it has been used to advance a false agenda. Furthermore, the fruits of science, as in technology, have been responsible for separating us more and more from nature, encouraging us to think of ourselves in terms of machines. The body is just a machine and the mind is just a computer. As for the soul, that, according to science, is just a product of material processes, a truly disastrous ideology that has accomplished more spiritual damage than practically anything else in modern times. Disbelieve this if you wish, but first remember the words of Jesus that we should not fear those who can kill the body so much as those who can kill the soul. The war against the soul is in full force at the moment. It is all the more effective as most of us are quite unaware that we are at war.

Then the devil has been active on the political scene, often inciting resentment and revolution throughout the world. But, and here is the difficulty, nothing he instigates or incites is unreservedly bad. Revolutions are often against oppression. Society has never been what it should be. So there is usually some good or seeming good that obscures the bad, and, while the net overall spiritual effect will be deleterious, the worldly or outer effect may appear beneficial, hence its appeal to those who deny the spiritual. It requires discrimination to sort this out and distinguish one from the other. It also requires an awakening of the heart which those drawn to politics, especially political struggle, rarely possess, these people being usually more interested in power and ideology than goodness and truth. Even if the initial impulse in these situations is founded on the desire to improve the lot of humanity, the devil can rapidly pervert that into directions that lead to spiritual loss. Science in itself is good, attempts to liberate humanity from oppression are good, but when these things are misdirected, as they have been, then the end result is very damaging from the higher perspective.

The second front that the devil has focused on is the corruption of religion and spirituality. Here again he has attacked in several areas. First, he has tried to distort our idea of beauty through the perversion of art, music and culture. Again, not everything he has been behind is wholly bad but we must look to the overall effect both of modern art and music. I am not saying anything as foolish as all contemporary artists and musicians work at the devil's behest. Many are creative personalities who seek to develop art and express truth as they understand it. However, if the genres they work in and the way in which they express themselves are what the Masters have called creatively destructive, then the harm is done. And, of course, some, because of their own inner moral and intellectual failings, do leave themselves open to diabolical influence. But still, even within these contemporary debased genres, there is room for good as well as bad for the spiritual powers do not just let the devil have the field all to himself. They try to remedy the situation by inspiring artists themselves, so again there is positive as well as negative. It might seem a complicated situation but nevertheless the cumulative effect of art and music and culture in general over the last century has not been spiritually positive. Indeed, where present day popular music is concerned, and music is a very powerful and influential force as pointed out by Plato amongst others, it's been overwhelmingly negative, despite earlier work in this genre having many positive qualities.

I once asked a Master about false prophets and was told that there were many people teaching half-truths at present but they were not all evil, some were doing work at their level. I remember being quite taken aback by this because evil is a strong word to use of anyone. But the Masters, despite being oceans of love, are not naïve sentimentalists. They know reality. There are false teachers who do promote false teachings, though usually with enough of truth in them to make them palatable to some people. This is different to those whose teachings do not entirely reflect truth but whose intentions nonetheless are good, the second category of the two above. After all, who does fully reflect truth? But the point is that the dark forces have sought to distort spiritual teachings both within and outside the main religions, and they have been able to operate through certain human beings who have rendered themselves susceptible to their influence through spiritual and intellectual pride. Though their efforts have not gone unchallenged, they have not been unsuccessful either.

I am speaking in general terms here. You must exercise your own intuition as to what are false teachings and what is imperfect but can still be helpful. This is a time when people have to learn active spirituality, which means we must develop our own spiritual faculties rather than rely on religion to give us all the answers. This may well be a reason why misleading doctrines and false prophets are permitted to flourish.

The devil is a liar and a deceiver. This we have been told. He is also a perverter of truth. Every time there has been any sign of a spiritual awakening, the dark forces have moved in to muddy the waters. In the 1960s they aborted the nascent spiritual revival with the sexual revolution. Later, when the New Age movement arose (it had been around before but came back to prominence in the 1970s) it was soon diverted away from proper spirituality into psychic channels, by which I mean a concern with phenomena and the inner side of creation rather than the Creator. Even the Green movement, which had a lot of potential at one time, was soon side-tracked into just another front for leftist ideology, with any spirituality largely of the Earth goddess variety, which basically just projects nature onto the spiritual world, seeing the latter in terms of the former, the fundamental error of modern pagans who, unwilling or unable to acknowledge genuine transcendence, substitute a false one in its place.

So the dark forces throughout the 20th century and up to the present time have attempted to corrupt and subvert ideas of beauty, goodness and truth. They have sought to undermine traditional institutions from both within and from outside, marriage being an excellent example, but all the time they have made it appear that the changes they have fomented have been advances, which in some cases they really have been and, in others, elements of them have been. But, once again, the overall spiritual effect is always negative and the trend is always downwards. You might say that we live today in a more tolerant and inclusive society but the fact is that we live in a society that has totally lost touch with its roots and with its intended goal. In which case, if we're more tolerant, so what? That's a poor bargain. Our standards of what is beautiful and good and true have declined dramatically, and our sense of spiritual purpose is virtually non-existent, having been replaced by a bland humanitarianism which tries to be all things to all men but essentially has no other motive than to increase pleasure and decrease suffering for the earthly self.

In all this the devil has been aided and abetted by people in the world, some of whom may have had evil motives themselves though the majority have either had mixed motives or misplaced good intentions which the devil has taken advantage of. But here I must say that, while motive is always important, ignorance of the (spiritual) law does not constitute a defence, and people who promote what we may rightly call sin, as in that which separates us from God and our true spiritual selves, will have to accept the consequences of their actions. It's not as if we do not have widely available teachings telling us the reality of the situation.

I've included this chapter for the simple reason that it describes a reality, one recognised by all traditional spiritual teachings but especially Christianity, whose destruction is undoubtedly the chief aim of the dark forces today. They know what most stands in their way. I realise this will be rejected by the majority of people, including many who regard themselves as spiritual, and branded as reactionary, melodramatic or even mad. I fear that just shows how much the modernist ideology has infected our minds, causing us to throw out the baby of spiritual truth with the bathwater of superstitious and wrong-headed reactions to it. For, while our contemporary ways of thinking surely have put right some of the wrongs of the past, they have also, and this is the subtlety of the devil, whom no one has ever called stupid, caused us to lose contact with something much more important, namely the reality of God and the understanding of what sort of God he is, one of love and truth, neither of which can be understood without the other as we saw in an earlier chapter. We may have improved certain matters on the horizontal plane but this is at the cost of the vertical plane, and that is an exchange which delights the dark forces. They are happy for us to be more tolerant if we are less discriminating. They don't care how content and comfortable we are in this world if we deny the spiritual truth of what we are. What does it benefit a man to gain the whole world and lose his soul? Is that an exchange you care to make?

Messengers from God

After darkness comes light. Before concluding this book, I need to return to what lies behind it, which is to say, those spiritual beings I have called Masters. I've never been entirely happy with this term but it was the commonly used one in the 20th century and has the connotation of master and disciple so is probably as good as any. Sometimes they would use it themselves but, when I asked them directly what/who they were, they told me to think of them as messengers from God, and that is what I did and still do. The word angel means messenger but I don't think they were angels. Obviously, any spiritually inclined person understands that angels do exist and perform various functions in the spiritual world depending on their position in the angelic hierarchy, ranging from the little elementals who are supposed to be behind many of the workings of nature, to the great archangels who basically run the universe. It is standard doctrine to say that where God can delegate, he does. And I see no reason to doubt the idea every human being has his or her guardian angel.

However, angels are supposed to be a separate creation, and I believe that the Masters were human beings in this world once who have now joined the company of saints in the heavenly worlds. They have achieved what we are still struggling to do. They are our elder brothers. Indeed, they did sometimes speak of themselves as brothers (which is not to say there are no female equivalents, there are). I know they spoke from the heavenly worlds because they said as much, describing themselves as living in a world where **all was poetry, music and colour.** On another occasion, one of them said he came to me **in a sea of azure blue and gold.** These descriptions are both taken from my records of the first year they spoke to me. Unfortunately, I took fewer notes thereafter and have lost those I did take, but

I remember they would sometimes mention the glory of their world in order to encourage me and stiffen my resolve to do my spiritual duty. At the same time, they needed me to come down to earth and not become a spiritual escapist, dreaming of heaven.

I mention this because it is a common failing of those entering on the spiritual path. Heaven is real. The spiritual realm is our true home. But we come to Earth to learn the lessons of Earth and that we will not do if we don't accept that here is where we are meant to be, for the time being at least. This is why suicide is regarded as wrong in religious circles. We have a duty to God and to our spiritual selves, and should not try to circumvent that. Generally, we have to deal with whatever life throws at us and have faith that it is either for our spiritual good, or a way in which we can serve God's greater purposes for the human race. We have been assured that those who suffer now will be more than recompensed later, hard as that may sometimes be to believe.

My understanding of the Masters is that they form part of a spiritual hierarchy that is dedicated to the upliftment and spiritual education of humanity. They have been through the experiences of this world, and come out of them triumphant. They have been crucified in Christ and risen with him. As humanity's forerunners, they are examples of what we should be aiming to become. Most souls who have achieved then progress to higher heavenly worlds far removed from this mortal plane, but some remain in the spiritual orbit of our world from where they serve humanity. The bulk of their work on an individual level will be with our souls, which remain in the higher worlds when we are born in this physical world (as they said, **the greater part of you remains with us and I can assure you that you wish this training to take place however difficult it may sometimes seem).** Thus they seek to inspire us on the level of intuition from whence messages will filter down to our conscious earthly minds. But sometimes they are able to take a more direct approach, and though I can't say how or why this would happen, I can vouch for the fact that it does. I do, though, feel bound to add that, in my view, the great majority of contacts made between people in this world and those in the next are not of this kind, whatever may be claimed. There is an abundance of spirits "on the other side", and most are not of this elevated level. Even setting aside demonic deceivers, there are many who, because they are in a spiritual world which is much more expanded in every respect than this world, consider themselves to be more spiritually advanced than they actually are. These are the ones that the average psychic, medium or channeller will encounter. From a Christian point of view, most of these would be in purgatorial worlds rather than true heavenly ones.

As for how an aspiring individual might contact the Masters, that is not up to us. If such a thing is meant to be, then it will be and that's all that can be said on the subject. What we can do is prepare the ground by making sure our spiritual motives are pure and our hearts properly inclined to the love of God. That is really as much as any of us can do, and it is all that is expected.

I said that the Masters seek to inspire us through the higher mind. They told me that when they no longer spoke to me outwardly, they would communicate in a different way. They also told me on several occasions that they tried to impress me with ideas which I would receive on the level of the intuition, though it was up to me to learn to discriminate between the truth of that and what they termed wishful thinking. This is something we all have to do since no one has perfect intuitive response. In each case this spiritual faculty will be responded to by the personal mind, until, that is, we have so disciplined and purified the mind for it to be a perfect receptor for spiritual truth. This is where devotion to truth and strict personal honesty come in.

The spiritual powers impress us on a higher plane and we translate that impression as best we can, according to the degree of our own receptivity. It is not the same thing as telepathy which operates on a lower level, a purely mental one. This process operates exclusively on the spiritual plane and requires a sensitivity to that plane on our part. Without that sensitivity, which is dependent to a large extent on inner purity and love of truth, we will not be able to respond to spiritual impression, though we may well respond to impressions from lower levels, which is why there is so much spiritual confusion in this world. And why it is often easier for false ideas to gain traction than true ones, necessarily more demanding in terms of our ability to live them. Eventually, though, the idea is that we develop ourselves the perfect insight, the conscious knowing truth by being truth, that arises naturally and spontaneously when we have aligned our inner nature with that of God and coordinated our will to his. This is not a passive thing like instinct but requires active engagement with divine reality.

It may be that there are genuine spiritual beings communicating directly with their disciples in this world nowadays, but I am not aware of such and from my own perspective the time for that is past. We are now responsible for ourselves and must seek to live from the highest position we can while under constant bombardment from the prince of this world, who has more or less taken over completely in terms of all aspects of the outer world. He dominates the political and cultural worlds, the educational and scientific ones, too, and he has corrupted most forms of religion and spirituality. I'm afraid that is just how things are. It does no good to avoid the reality.

But we are not alone. The spiritual world is always with us and seeks to inspire us, but we must cleanse our hearts and minds to be able to detect this. We must stand aside from "this world" but not disdain it or our fellow men and women, even when they are in thrall to the enemy (let's call a spade a spade). They are God's children just as we are. He wants to bring them to him, however far they wander but, ultimately, it is their choice.

God forces no one.

So, listen for the voice within. Blot out the noise of this world, however persuasive and confident it sounds. Know that the darkness of this time was prophesied and so was the light that eventually follows after. Keep faithful, watch and pray and don't worry if you appear to be alone. You may be heavily outnumbered but you are not alone. Through enduring this period of trial, you have the opportunity of making greater progress than you might have done living in a more spiritually congenial time. You are being forced back on yourself because there is very little out there that is reliable. This is a test but it is also a chance to develop your spiritual nature to a higher level. It's like developing a muscle. The heavier the weight you struggle against, the more that muscle will grow. Within reason, of course, but the Masters are there to ensure that the bounds of possibility are not exceeded. Lift your mind up to their level through prayer and meditation and they will be there to support you. But remember when you do that, they are servants themselves, servants of God who is their Master. They would be the first to say that.

How to Remember

We have talked about the love of God in these pages as the essential factor in spiritual development, but here we might consider what that actually means. How can we know that what we think is the love of God really is that? For, after all, history shows us that many people claim to love God when what is really going on is that they have an attachment to their own idea of God.

It is not uncommon to have an image of God that is either of our own making or else derives at second hand from the religion we follow. And then we claim that our attachment to that is love when really it is just a personal preference or emotional response to something that gives us comfort. Often it doesn't even affect our behaviour radically. So there are two things to take into account here. One is God and the other is love. If we say we have love for God, is it really love we have and is it really for God?

Well, this is something that only God can know for sure but from our perspective we can say that the difference between God and an idea about God is the difference between what is known in the heart and what comes from the mind. Where is our notion of God held, head or heart, in thought or through intuition and, if intuition, is that pure and free of prejudice, preconception and the host of lower impulses that the mind is subject to? In other words, is our connection to God just to an idea we have about God or is it to something real beyond our self which we sense because we have started to look beyond our self?

I would say we can truly perceive something of God in three ways. One is through religion. If a particular revelation speaks to us we can intuit something of God through that revelation. True, we may get caught up in the form of that religion, its outer aspect, but, if our heart is pure and our aspiration sincere, we should be able to see through the form to the inner truths behind it, and use the form without being bound by it.

Then we can understand something of the reality of God through nature, while remembering that God is in nature yet always remains transcendent to it. But for those who believe in God, everything in the world is a sign indicating him and the way he works. It's a fallen world so not everything is a perfect sign but still Creation is a book which, when you learn how to read it, points to its Creator and gives you an insight into his mind. We can see his presence in the sun, the sky and so on. These are symbols that inform us about the metaphysical principles that lie behind them. In addition, we can perceive God's laws and, through them, see him operating through the way the world works. The beauty of nature also tells us about its Creator.

Finally, we can know God in the heart. He is present in us as our very being and we are connected to him through the heart. However, to know this consciously demands a degree of purity that can only be acquired through hard spiritual effort. It requires a simplicity that is not afraid to seem foolish, and it requires humility. If you turn to God without having first turned away from yourself, you will fall into illusion, and whatever you find, and you may well find something you think is spiritual, it won't be God.

True awareness of God comes from seeing that there is something greater than you that is the source of all that is good and beautiful and true. This awareness inspires a love that brings about complete dedication, the desire to serve and the ability to sacrifice. There is perfect acceptance of God's will, which means that we accept our experiences without resistance while, at the same time, looking for ways in which we might serve that will. It might be said that some of this could equally apply to the religious fanatic but the difference once again is between head and heart. The true lover of God does God's will in a spirit of acceptance and humble gratitude. The fanatic, obsessed with his idea of God, always uses force of some kind.

God is within and God is without and God has been revealed through the great religions, most completely in the person of Christ. However, unless we know him in our hearts, there is the strong possibility we will replace the reality with our concept of it and so, in a sense, become an idol worshipper. Only through purification of heart and mind can we can start to disperse the clouds of self-centredness that block out God's light, and begin to perceive something of the living truth that lies behind all ideas about it. That very perception will bring love because it is of love.

The spiritual path has stages which have been expressed in various ways. These are stages we all have to go through, and an understanding of them will help to ease our ascent. Here I would like to look at them as they are expressed in terms of Sufism, though really, they are more or less exactly the same in Christianity. Who influenced whom in this respect is an interesting question but not one I am qualified to answer, though I would always point to the Gospels as a primary source for the ideas expressed here. I do believe that the Sufis inherited the idea of love from the Christians, since there is not so much for them to go on in that regard in their holy book. In my view Islam, whatever its virtues, was a return to Old Testament ideas of religion and thus several steps down in spiritual terms from Christianity and the New Testament, never mind its misunderstanding and rejection of Christ as the Son of God. Sufism was an attempt to correct that and to introduce a mysticism of love to a religion of law. That's why it's still regarded with suspicion within some orthodox Muslim circles.

The stages are as follows:

Conversion and repentance.

This is the necessary first step. It is the acknowledgement that we have not been walking in the light of God, and the determination to change our ways. Conversion is not just adopting a new belief system. It means a complete uprooting of our old ways of thinking and doing, and an opening up of the heart and mind to hitherto denied realities. Repentance means a deep and sincere regret of our previous sinful ways, based on a real recognition of them and how they are an insult to our Maker. This is not self-hatred for, at the same time, we accept that we are made in God's image so that, when we turn to him, we can start to become like him. That is a long journey though. There is no point being deceived on that account, and thinking conversion and repentance are anything more than the start of a road that leads uphill and through some hard terrain before we get to the top of the mountain. Nevertheless, the beginning of a journey is, in many respects, the most important part.

Fear of the Lord.
This is fear in the sense of the overwhelming recognition of the power and glory of the Creator, and the appreciation that he is the source of our being. So not fear as in being frightened but a recognition that there is something so far above us as to make our own little ego insignificant. Again, though, this is a matter of insight into reality, so it includes the knowledge that we are loved for ourselves, though not so much for who we think we are as who we really are. Really, it means humility in the face of something we know to be much greater than us. Fear is the cure for pride.

Detachment.
This is the understanding that God is reality and this world subsists entirely in him. He should be the focus of our thoughts and desires, not anything that lies in the created world and is not him. We do not have to reject creation but we do have to see it as secondary. Detachment means not having idols of any kind, not setting our thoughts or desires on objects which can be physical or mental. We seek the Subject.

Poverty.
This is letting go of worldly concerns and being content with little. It is connected to detachment and it leads to freedom. Ultimately we will find that we have access to everything, but to reach that stage we must learn to desire nothing. This word desire sometimes causes misunderstanding. A person devoid of desire is dead. Desire is immature love. So enjoyment of God's gifts is not wrong at all, but it should be a non-grasping desire that is able to enjoy spontaneously without seeking to repeat or prolong an experience, or reduce it to egotistic self-seeking or satisfaction.

Patience.
Patience means acceptance of God's will and knowing that where you are and what you experience is what you need here and now. It is waiting on God's good time and not trying to force his hand. It is being able to live in the moment without trying to turn that into the future. In essence, it is knowing that God is always with you, even if you can't detect him, and so all will be well.

Self-surrender.
Give yourself entirely to God. This is the precursor to union. You must let go of self, holding nothing back, and open your heart fully to God, your Creator. It is a kind of self-emptying but not in the sense of an annihilation or denial of self, but of a gift of self. You are returning what God gave you to him and he will give it back filled with himself. Self-surrender might require looking foolish in the eyes of the world, but that is all part of the test of how much you are prepared to give of yourself: some or all. You must give all because if you retain anything of yourself, you have effectively retained everything.

Union with God.
The final stage of the spiritual journey: the union of the individual soul with the Universal Soul. But it is not the abstract thing that might suggest nor is it an absorption, a "dewdrop slipping into the shining sea". Or rather the dewdrop does slip into the sea but it retains its "dewdropness", and the sea is not a vast cosmic ocean of impersonal life but the living God of love and goodness and truth. Thus the fruits of incarnation and experience of the material world are retained, not simply let go and abandoned as though they had never been. The self, purified and transformed, is united with God, and the journey from spirit to matter and back to spirit is complete but the individual self remains as a glorified new creation. The end is the beginning but with all the benefits of the journey made between the two. Initial oneness is made more by its transformation into love.

Those are the stages in the spiritual journey, according to the mystical path of Sufism, with my commentaries on them. I would say the Christian way is no different, and I would also say that a Christian theology makes more sense of this path of love than the Islamic one and has probably been a strong influence on it. But really labels are unimportant. What matters is the sincere attempt to tread the spiritual path, together with the knowledge that this will always require a rebirth which must inevitably be preceded by a death. So do not fear death but see it as the gateway to greater life.

The two most important weapons in the spiritual aspirant's armoury are prayer and meditation. These are how we approach God in his transcendent and immanent aspects, both of which we must do if we would know him. It therefore makes sense, as we approach the end of this book, to briefly examine how we can use these two methods in our attempt to remember the Creator.

Prayer has various forms. There is the petitionary sort, in which you might ask God for something, perhaps his help for yourself or others in difficult circumstances or else just his grace. Then there is prayer as thanksgiving in which you express your gratitude to the Creator for his blessings and his love, or maybe just for the fact that he has given you life. Above all, though, prayer is a way of remembering God. Let's face it, as we go about our daily business we often, even the most devout among us, forget God. Much as we might wish to, we simply don't consciously live and move and have our being in him. We are frail creatures and we forget. Prayer is important as an act of remembering. It is a way of practicing the presence of God, which is the most important of spiritual exercises.

There is also the fact that prayer is beneficial as a humbling experience. We are on our knees before our Maker, metaphorically as well as physically. We don't have to kneel physically in order to pray but that is a position which encourages an attitude of humility. We are humbling ourselves before something greater than ourself but doing so in a way that, unlike some other postures of prayer, is not abasing oneself like a slave before its despotic overlord. Humility does not mean making yourself insignificant and worthless. God would not create a thing without worth, and if you think you are worthless then you must think everyone else is, too. But it is recognising the fact that you are a created being and acknowledging your Creator appropriately. With humility there is the possibility, even likelihood, of love but with self-abasement, fear is more probable.

If prayer involves addressing oneself to the transcendent God then meditation is more to do with the God within. Again, there are various types of meditation but I would reduce them to those with or without form. Meditation with form might involve focusing on an image of deity, the figure of Christ being an obvious example, in the attempt to draw close to him and absorb something of his spiritual quality. It could also be contemplation of a symbol that has spiritual significance, say a lily for purity or pink rose for selfless love, but the sun as an image of the God within could also serve. These act as a focus to still wandering thoughts, as well as attuning the meditator to an inner spiritual reality.

The stilling of thought is one of the principal purposes of meditation. The constant movement of the mind should be arrested so that silence can be known and peace found. Such is meditation without form. However this is not in itself a spiritual thing, and theoretically a non-believer can do it as well as a believer. That is why there needs to be the sense of dedication to a higher power in order to change a psychological act to a spiritual one. Motive is all important. It is not like a scientific experiment in which the intent of the experimenter is irrelevant. The intent is crucial to lift meditation to a higher plane. Otherwise it remains in the realm of therapy, effective on one level, but unable to bring its practitioner closer to the true God.

Prayer is remembering God. It is aimed at God Transcendent. Meditation is contemplation. It is directed to God Immanent. Christian meditation is contemplation of God or Christ with the idea of entering into the divine presence. It must be accompanied by an attitude of love and humility which is what I think marks it out from some other forms, though I realise practitioners of these other forms would not necessarily agree. But I do feel there is a qualitative difference between theistic meditation and non-theistic kinds and, though the latter can bring some profound rewards and realisations, it is the former that takes one to a higher reality, one in which the meditator can arrive at a real relationship with God rather than remain resting in his own soul. Let us say that the active union of the soul with God in love is a greater thing than that of the soul simply resting at the deepest level of its own being.

Prayer and meditation exist as spiritual practices in all religions and there are broad similarities between them, even if they are not identical. In Christianity, until recently, meditation or contemplation was largely restricted to the monastery, that's to say those individuals who wished to develop a deeper relationship with God. For the layman, prayer was generally enough and even then it was mostly the petitionary, confessionary or thanksgiving sort. But, while prayer enables us to speak to God and remember him as our Creator, it is meditation on him or his qualities that can bring us into closer communion with him. For by silencing the worldly mind, whether through focus on a sacred image or otherwise, God's holy presence can begin to percolate into our conscious existence and transform us from a creature of this world into one who will someday be worthy to take his or her place in the kingdom of souls in heaven.

You might say that prayer orientates our mind to God but proper contemplation on him invites him into our heart.

Teaching for a Child

For my final chapter I would like to, as it were, go back to the beginning. Anyone who has children must be concerned with their education and, for a believer in the reality of God, it is their spiritual education that is the most important, especially in the contemporary world, when that is almost completely neglected. Isn't it a strange society that insists on sex education for very young children but does nothing for spiritual education? I am not criticising instructing children on the nature of their bodies but they should be made aware of the reality of their whole being, and see how the different parts that comprise it relate to each other: the place each part, body, soul and spirit, has in the overall scheme of things. Taking a part out of context cannot fail to give it disproportionate meaning and significance, and even give a totally false idea of it.

So, teaching our children what they are and giving them an understanding of their place in the world, of their duties to others and, most of all, to God is essential. The past was ignorant in many respects but it was wise in the most important way. It recognised a Creator and knew that this world was not man's true home. He was here for a purpose, and that was not to make money or even live a nominally good and fulfilling life. It was to fit himself for eternity. Now we have this extraordinary situation in which the most educated people are frequently the most ignorant because they don't understand that basic truth, having been trained to regard it as outdated and foolish. They have been so educated on a purely intellectual level that their minds are closed to anything higher. It's an irony that universities arose from monasteries but have now so severed their links with the spiritual that they have cut themselves off from the truth and frequently propagate its opposite, thereby deforming young minds.

If you told anyone that modern education was narrower

in scope than at any time in history, they would react with astonishment. How can that be when the range of subjects is greater than ever, and the depth of knowledge, especially scientific, is such that it makes the understanding of previous generations look like the investigations of children? But there is really only one subject taught today and that is materialism. That's the assumed background to everything, even the arts (nearly all modern arts are blasphemy, the Masters have said). Yes, contemporary knowledge is hugely impressive but it is, as the cliché goes, more and more about less and less. I do not decry this knowledge, neither do I reject worldly learning, but it should be supplementary to the knowledge of God not a replacement for it because, unless it is seen in the light of the knowledge of God, it is not really knowledge at all. Rather it is sophisticated ignorance.

Really education should mostly be about the education of the soul, and if that is not given a central position in a child's education, or an adult's for that matter, the person remains uneducated and ignorant. Unfortunately this is the case with the majority of those who set the agenda today whether they be politicians, scientists, artists, teachers or leaders in almost any field you care to mention. Such people are usually highly educated but know nothing of what actually matters. Consequently their influence is destructive and is inevitably leading to a society and culture that has divorced itself from reality, which means, whatever the appearances, it is on the path to disintegration.

With that in mind, I would like to run through what I believe all children should be taught, almost before they are taught anything else. This should be the backdrop against which all their future education is framed.

Spiritual truth is quite simple or, at any rate, its fundamentals are. This is something my teachers always insisted on. In their words, **spiritual truth is simple but it is easy to get lost in philosophical speculations which lead nowhere.** Now this means that basically a child should be able to understand the essential truths about existence, about where it comes from, what its duties are and what its destiny should be. Obviously not in detail but sufficiently to be able to lead a life in harmony with the universe instead of one completely at odds with it as is mostly the case nowadays.

So what are the essentials which every child should be taught? Different cultures might emphasise different aspects of the story and present them in slightly differing forms, but I would say that any child entering this world who is not given the information below is deprived of its birthright, and sent out into life already partially crippled in spirit. There is no need to develop these ideas to begin with. That can come later, as and when required. The simple understanding of basic truths is enough to start off with. A child may reject these truths. He or she has that right and nothing should be forced. But not to give the child access to them from an early age is a form of cruelty to a growing and developing mind. This is not indoctrination (if it were then refusing to do it would be equally so) and it should not be something that is insisted on but a gentle presentation of fundamental truths for the child's consideration and pondering.

Here is what I believe each child should be taught when it begins to ask questions about the world in which it finds itself.

- There is a Creator. God exists and God is a person. He loves you.
- You have an immortal soul for which you are responsible. It is cherished as a unique individual.
- All life is one as it all comes from God and is held within his keeping. However, all forms of life are different and, though they are not all equal as they appear in the world, they should all be respected and valued.
- There is a divine order of being and we should try to ob-

serve that and conform ourselves to it, not only because it is the truth but because we will be happier that way.

- This Earth is a spiritual school and we are here to learn lessons, some of which may be difficult and even painful. We have to understand that, and not think that because of occasional hardship that God has abandoned us or does not exist. These are the chisellings that turn a block of wood into a beautiful statue.
- There are forces of darkness but this is nothing to be frightened about. They have no power that God could not extinguish in a second and they cannot hurt us or influence us in any way unless we let them by listening to their false counsel, which always goes against what we know in our hearts, though it may appeal to the selfish or proud or lazy part of us. They are allowed to exist because they give us an opportunity to be tested.
- We live in a time when spiritual truths are being lost but our task is not to be misled by that. We have to have faith which is based on the highest truths we have been taught plus what we sense in our hearts when we are loyal to the best we know.

One could certainly add to this list but I didn't want to make it too long or too complicated or too specific. One could mention that God has messengers who sometimes come to teach us the truth about him. And one could say that the current views about men and women being descended from animals are by no means proven and, even if they were correct, would still only relate to our bodies not our souls, which are from heaven. From my personal perspective, I would want to add something about Jesus Christ as, at the very least, the divine exemplar, but I've tried to make this as universally applicable as possible. I'm not saying Christ isn't universally applicable. I absolutely believe he is but he is not perceived as such by everybody, and this is intended to be just a general outline attesting to the reality of the spiritual world. It's a framework to be built on later.

Conclusion

The theme of this book has been the reality of God. I have considered various spiritual approaches that do away with God, either literally as in Buddhism or to all intents and purposes as in Advaita, and said why I think that, despite their virtues, they are incomplete. After all, if the goal is something like the impersonal state of bliss they teach, why would we ever be born in this world with all its attendant sorrow and suffering? But we come to this earth in a body and with a mind because it is here, partly because of the sorrow and suffering, that we can become aware of goodness, beauty and truth, and coordinate our being to those realities. If the object of the spiritual quest was the obliteration of self, why would we have this self, which is a real, non-phenomenal thing not a mental construction? Why not avoid all the illusion and unpleasantness associated with life on this planet and remain in eternal bliss? The answer is that there is something better than bliss, and that is the fullness of love which can only be known by an individual. Impersonal bliss no doubt exists in some form, but the fullness of reality is personal, and the exploration of that is the reason for creation and everything in it.

We have also looked at atheism and various objections to God because of the existence of suffering. Atheism is fundamentally incoherent. It assumes wholes are no more than the sum of their parts, and that the greater comes from the lesser. It explains nothing and can only be believed by ignoring vast chunks of our experience, both of the world and of ourselves. Moreover, I think it could really only take effect in the minds of beings leading a largely unnatural existence in a largely artificial environment. The reality of God cannot be conclusively proved because it's not meant to be, but it is known in our hearts so all we have to do is listen without prejudice.

Suffering and the problem of evil can also lead people to doubt the existence of a Creator. But rather than the problem of evil, why not consider the problem of good? Or the problem of beauty. Evil and ugliness are not truths in themselves but defacements of truths, just as you can't knock something down without having built it up first. The teaching of the Fall answers the question of where these imperfections came from. It also helps to explain the origin of suffering, though that has a teaching purpose, too, hard as we often find that to accept, trapped as we are in the here and now. But from the standpoint of the eternal, it becomes less important, glib as that may seem to the non-believer exclusively identified with his mind and body.

Science has liberated human beings from the drudgery of earlier ages, though factory workers of the past and office workers of the present might not always agree. But, even when we accept that it has, there can be no doubt that it has also narrowed our vision. It has trapped us in this material world, both because that is the domain of its knowledge and also because that is where its technological achievements lie. The more we use and become dependent on these, the more our consciousness becomes limited to the domain in which they operate. Their usefulness and power and extent to which they work their "magic" thus become spiritually dangerous. They cut us off from the higher parts of our nature. You only have to look at people, especially young people, glued to their mobile phones to realise that. But this is just the latest in a long line of developments. There is little we can do about it, such is the way of the world, but we can at least become aware of it and restrict our own use, as well as try to engage our minds as much as possible with the real world, both inner and outer.

Human beings, though fallen, are intrinsically good or, at least, want to be. We are also intrinsically religious. The devil knows this and exploits it to our spiritual disadvantage. He knows few would follow a path of obvious evil and therefore he constructs a path of false good to lead us away from the true good. Now, it must be understood that if we were rightly ordered we would not follow this path, but it is subtly designed and so seems fair to those whose hearts are not quite in the right place, that is to say, orientated to God. This is the path of apparent worldly good, separated from God, indeed separated from any spirituality at all except, when necessary, a false spirituality that, if analysed, is usually to do with self-fulfilment. This, I must tell you, is the path of the modern left and all that derives from it. In truth, the devil plays for both sides and often acts as referee as well, but principally it is through the left that he has first subverted and then inverted the Good, the Beautiful and the True, and sought to turn Nature on her head over the course of the last hundred years. The devil hates both God and Nature, and is doing his best to turn us against them, too. He wants to make good appear evil and evil good but he does it with great cunning. He's done it before. According to Tertullian when Nero martyred the early Christians, it was on the grounds of hatred for humanity.

The real power behind the left has always had as its goal the undermining and destruction of proper religion. Clearly it has to replace that with something else, since humanity does have a religious instinct. What it has chosen is a secular religion based on an ideology of the oneness of humanity as it exists in this world, a world severed from God and without any sense of the transcendent. So basically, it has made politics into a religion, which is why I have to attack it in these pages instead of ignoring it, which is what I would prefer to do. But when Caesar invades God's realm and the political tries to usurp the prerogatives of the spiritual, then the spiritual person cannot pretend a lofty indifference and position himself above it all. When the world becomes a spiritual war zone, one has to pick a side. The side I have picked is not right against left but spiritual against worldly. The left has long sought to make a world without God, and the right has just followed in its footsteps and effectively become it in all that matters from a higher perspective. It, too, has settled for atheistic relativism. A true right would have as its focus the reality of God, and all else would come from that. Of course, even this can be corrupted but that would mean the reality of God had been replaced by an image of God, an idol to all intents and purposes, and so the spiritual had been materialised and the mind taken over what belongs to the heart.

Jesus said not a dot will pass from the Law until all is accomplished. In this he was clearly conservative. But still he built on the Law, it was not set entirely in stone, and in this he was progressive. The modern left seeks to build the future on the destruction of the Law and that is why it must be resisted. But any reactionary right that wants to turn the clock back must also be resisted. The truth is in neither of them but a proper spiritual awareness that seeks to cultivate an active relationship with God, and develop a true connection to divine being.

All of which brings us back to Christ, but then we must always come back to him. That is one of the major themes of this book. He is relevant not just for Christians or even the Western world, but for all humanity. His advent changed the world and our spiritual possibilities in an absolutely fundamental way. There are other religious teachers, prophets and sages but Christ is the perfect archetype of which they are but representatives, and any spiritual path which does not have him at its centre will always be incomplete. This does not mean that all must outwardly be followers of Jesus Christ, but the truths that he manifested and established in this world, and which, to a greater or lesser degree, and either directly or through a kind of spiritual osmosis, permeated into every other religion, must be known and lived. Inwardly we must all be disciples of the risen Christ.

This is because Christ was more than an avatar (descent of a spiritual being from the heavenly world) or a Buddha, an awakened, enlightened human. He redeemed mankind by offering a way to transform the fallen self and the world of nature rather than simply seek liberation from them (as was the highest path before him). The way to salvation offered by Christ was, and still is, through love and sacrifice. It is by these means that the worlds of spirit and matter, sundered since the Fall, can be brought back together again and made one in perfect harmony. This is first accomplished in the individual and then, one day, will be so collectively with the new heaven and new earth, as prophesied in the Book of Revelation.

A Final Word

The self is a prison from which we all yearn to escape. But, at the same time, it is also that which frees us from fate and necessity, and opens us up to the reality of love. How can we reconcile these two things? There is only one way and that is through God.

What is the difference between the self-hatred of the nihilist and the recognition that he is a sinner of the saint? Both are reacting to the reality of their selfhood and its enclosed nature in different ways, but one reacts from the self itself while the other reacts from awareness of a truth beyond the self.

The difference is that between despair and hope, hatred and love, denial and faith. It is the difference between the refusal to see there is anything more than the me of the nihilist, and the trust in a higher power of the saint. The nihilist rejects while the sinner accepts. The one is closed while the other is open.

But why even say nihilist and saint, why go to extremes? The exact same contrast exists between the atheist and the believer. When all is said and done, these are the two types of human being and this is the major line of demarcation between human beings.

Whence arises this difference between the two types? The answer is that in the one there is the trace, however small it may be, of humility and love, while in the other there is pride and denial. Of course, we all have these contradictory elements within us but it is the side we incline to in our hearts that makes the difference.

So I would say that the atheist denies and rejects because of pride while the believer accepts because of love. Perhaps this sounds too simplistic but there is still something to be said for reducing complexities and mixed motivations to their simplest state because then we get down to basic truths and the reality of the heart.

When our teachers assess our spiritual state, it is to the heart they look. An open heart is open to God but a closed heart denies God. However moral you may be in the eyes of the world, if you deny God your heart is closed. It really is that simple. That doesn't mean you can't have doubts. Doubts are natural and even, to an extent, healthy, in that they can allow for growth and prevent faith from calcifying, but they should be in the overall context of faith. Faith in God is the mark of a person whose heart is aligned with truth.

God the Creator is real. He dwells in the innermost depths of your heart and above the highest heaven. He is your Father and he is Being itself. His name is I AM and his nature is love. He sits with you as you read these lines. Remember him.

Also by William Wildblood:

Meeting the Masters, Axis Mundi Books

AXIS MUNDI
BOOKS

Axis Mundi Books
EXPLORING THE WORLD OF HIDDEN KNOWLEDGE

Axis Mundi Books provide the most revealing and coherent explorations and investigations of the world of hidden or forbidden knowledge. Take a fascinating journey into the realm of Esoteric Mysteries, High Magic (non-pagan), Mysticism, Mystical Worlds, Goddess, Angels, Aliens, Archetypes, Cosmology, Alchemy, Gnosticism, Theosophy, Kabbalah, Secret Societies and Religions, Symbolism, Quantum Theory, Conspiracy Theories, Apocalyptic Mythology, Unexplained Phenomena, Holy Grail and Alternative Views of Mainstream Religion.

If you have enjoyed this book, why not tell other readers by posting a review on your preferred book site?

Recent bestsellers from Axis Mundi Books are:

On Dragonfly Wings

A Skeptic's Journey to Mediumship

Daniela I. Norris

Daniela Norris, former diplomat and atheist, discovers communication with the other side following the sudden death of her younger brother.

Paperback: 978-1-78279-512-4 ebook: 978-1-78279-511-7

Inner Light

The Self-Realization via the Western Esoteric Tradition

P.T. Mistlberger

A comprehensive course in spiritual development using the powerful teachings of the Western esoteric tradition.

Paperback: 978-1-84694-610-3 ebook: 978-1-78279-625-1

The Seeker's Guide to Harry Potter

Dr Geo Trevarthen

An in-depth analysis of the mythological symbols and themes encountered in the Harry Potter series, revealing layers of meaning beneath the surface of J K Rowling's stories.

Paperback: 978-1-84694-093-4 ebook: 978-1-84694-649-3

The 7 Mysteries

Your Journey from Matter to Spirit

Grahame Martin

By simply reading this book you embark on a journey of transformation from the world of matter into spirit.

Paperback: 978-1-84694-364-5

Angel Healing & Alchemy
How To Begin Melchisadec, Sacred Seven & the Violet Ray
Angela McGerr
Angelic Healing for physical and spiritual harmony.
Paperback: 978-1-78279-742-5 ebook: 978-1-78279-337-3

Colin Wilson's 'Occult Trilogy'
A Guide for Students
Colin Stanley
An essential guide to Colin Wilson's major writings on the occult.
Paperback: 978-1-84694-706-3 ebook: 978-1-84694-679-0

The Heart of the Hereafter
Love Stories from the End of Life
Marcia Brennan
This book can change not only how we view the end of life, but how we view life itself and the many types of love we experience.
Paperback: 978-1-78279-528-5 ebook: 978-1-78279-527-8

Kabbalah Made Easy
Maggy Whitehouse
A down to earth, no-red-strings-attached look at the mystical tradition made famous by the Kabbalah Center.
Paperback: 978-1-84694-544-1 ebook: 978-1-84694-890-9

The Whole Elephant Revealed
Insights Into the Existence and Operation of Universal Laws and the Golden Ratio
Marja de Vries
An exploration of the universal laws which make up the dynamic harmony and balance of the universe.
Paperback: 978-1-78099-042-2 ebook: 978-1-78099-043-9